THE ROGUE'S GUIDE

TO

TANGIER

By "Bert and Mabel" Winter

Illustrations

by

Salowa Skiredj

With Best Wishes from the Rogue (author)

Gordon "Bert" Winter

Tangier　　　　1986

Tangier office address c/o G. ISERRA, Post Box 641,
Tanger.

Printed by Etei-Nord, Zone Industrielle, Route de Tétouan
- B.P. 101 - Tanger - (Maroc).

Contents

INTRODUCTION TO TANGIER

Tangier is quite definitely one of the most unusual cities in the world. A weird and wonderful place which is so mind-bogglingly different that some short-stay tourists leave saying they will never return. In most cases they were unable to cope with the difference because nobody had time to explain this different world to them.

And that is what this book is all about. When you have read it you will be an instant Fundi on Tangier. That is guaranteed because, as you will see at the end, many experts on Tangier helped us to compile all the fascinating information. You will glean scores of little known facts and a treasure trove of valuable snippets explaining just what makes this amazing city tick.

Racy, witty and highly informative, The Rogue introduces you to a host of local personalities and characters. It also tells you how to find Mr Madini, the smelliest man in town, how to spot Seashell Sam, Robert the Ringer, Caffeine Colin, Charlie Brown, Foghorn Fred and how to meet Mustapha, the amazing one-armed "Lighter King". You also get an introduction to Aisha, the most beautiful and elusive lady in town. ENJOY YOUR HOLIDAY.

Hints and Wrinkles

The first thing most tourists go looking for on arrival in Tangier is a street map and, quite often, they pay through the nose for it. But you can get one completely free, in English, French, Spanish or German, from the Official Tourist Office at 29 Boulevard Pasteur.

The Boulevard Pasteur is the main street in this city and at the end of it is another central landmark, the Cafe de Paris. Apart from being Tangier's most famous coffee rendezvous, the Cafe de P is an important place to go looking for because it is often the starting point used by this book when advising you how to get to other interesting places.

After a few days sightseeing and getting to know Tangier, many tourists wish they could get to know a Moroccan family as well. Not many succeed in this because they are either too shy or just don't know how to go about it. The answer is quite simple. Every good hotel in this city has at least one young employee who would be tickled pink to invite you to his home in the Kasbah.

All you need to do is choose the waiter or barman you like best and get talking to him on a personal level. Steer the conversation round to his family and ask if he lives with his mother. Does his mother go out to work or is she a housewife ? From his answers you should be able to judge the quality of your man and the odds are very strong that he will offer to take you to his home when he is off duty.

But before going, tell him it's an old Western custom to take a present when you are going to meet someone's family. There's a good reason for this. When you get to his home, however poor they may be, the family will almost certainly shower you with kindness, mint tea and perhaps a meal of Cous Cous.

Some tourists feel so overwhelmed by this that they offer money as a token of their gratitude, which may not be a tactful thing to do. That's why we suggest you buy a present. But what kind and how much should it cost ? This is not really difficult to assess if you did your detective work well while questioning your new-found friend about his family.

If you suspect they are not rich, it's a great idea to let him guide you to a butcher where you can buy a kilo of beef or lamb because meat is always a terrific present. But not pork, of course. If you guess the family is well off, a cake   is a good solution and you can hand it to the mother on arrival.

Make sure you have no holes in your socks, Bert, because in many Moroccan homes they remove their shoes in the hallway. Ignore those Mills and Boon type stories which suggest you will be offered raw sheep's eyes to swallow whole. That's as unlikely as meeting Barbara Cartland's handsome virgin Prince mounted on a dazzlingly Omo-white stallion.

To visit a Moroccan home and not be offered tea is unthinkable. It's a traditional mark of respect and hospitality. The only difference is that Moroccans drink mint tea and the process of preparing it is a lengthy ritual which gives the host time to gently explore and assess your personality.

Don't let that scare you. Moroccans are not abrasive. To them, conversation is truly an art form when entertaining guests and they are

2

past masters at making you feel at home. They rarely talk about themselves unless asked directly, but often start the conversation by asking you what you think of Tangier. Are you enjoying your holiday ? Do you have any problems and if so, how can they help to solve them ? Talk, and the gentle interchange of viewpoints slowly strengthens, just like thé tea as it's brewing, and you quickly realise that Moroccans play it very low key and rarely compete aggressively in conversation.

Cultured Moroccans are most unassuming. As you approached your host's home in the Kasbah you might have noticed that the walls outside were unpretentious. Just covered in a simple whitewash. No matter how well off the family is and how well furnished the house is on the inside, the outside is nearly always simple and anonymous.

The idea is not to arouse envy in the eyes of the neighbour because, in the Kasbah, a very rich man often lives next to a poor family. This sophisticated art of playing it low key is rather different to those Joneses back home who are always trying to keep up with us.

Back to mint tea. Smack your lips in loud appreciation when the father of the house gives you the first glass to taste after pouring it with dazzling accuracy from a teapot held high. After the tea you might be offered food, particularly if you brought meat as a present. In many cases you will squat on the carpet or a cushion and eat from a.large dish in the centre of a low table. Some families eat with their hands. It's much more fun than knives and forks although some Moroccans realise that Westerners find eating with their hands rather awkward and offer them spoons. If you opt to eat with your hands, remember that Moroccans use their right hand when eating and it is wise to copy them. Even if you are left-handed.

Another thing to keep in mind is that although they speak Arabic, Moroccans do not actually regard themselves as Arabs. They were here long before the Arabs arrived in the year 705 and they have seen many foreign tribes come and go. That includes the Phoenicians, the Greeks, Romans, Turks, Vandals, British, Portuguese, Spanish and French. Moroccans, though they have adopted some of the better aspects of the above cultures, still retain their own special brand of individuality. On the other hand, should you make a mistake in a Moroccan home, don't worry. They rarely tell you that you have done something wrong. And even if they do, it will be done so skilfully that you will take it as a compliment.

Yes, Tangier can be quite complicated for us Westerners. The basic thing to keep in mind is that life here really is different. Rudyard Kipling summed it up neatly by pointing out that East is East, West is West and never the twain shall meet. Both sides often find it difficult to fully comprehend the thought processes of the other as each side considers the other has a strange reverse way of thinking.

Most tourists arrive here firmly convinced that their country, religion, morals and social laws are the best in the world and some fail to consider the simple fact that Moroccans believe exactly the same about their country and their way of life. Bearing all that in mind, one quickly realises that Tangier is one of the few places in the world where East meets West so vividly and where the twain certainly manage to live happily side by side, with both sides showing tolerance to the other man and his different point of view. Race riots are unknown here and Tangier does not need a Race Relations Act.

As you can clearly see, people of all colours co-exist harmoniously in this city where people are mainly judged by their behaviour, not the colour of their skins.

We now turn to one tricky aspect which usually confronts tourists staying at good class hotels in Tangier. Walking out of the front door they find themselves ambushed by an ever vigilant phalanx of street salesmen offering garments, rugs, leather goods and various tourist trinkets. These chaps are astonishingly persistent and keep offering their wares even though you shake your head and say No.

This can be aggravating and some tourists show their annoyance by scowling or being rude. This is totally self-defeating. Be rude and he will retaliate with rudeness. He may be poor or even uneducated but, more often than not, he will have a great command of languages which he will use to stunning effect to combat your insults.

There is only one weapon you can use. That is a huge smile accompanied by the often repeated words, No Thank You. If you want to give him the impression that you are not a first day tourist, say Thank You in Arabic which, pronounced Shookran, is a magical word when said with a shake of the head and a smile. And the word La, with another big smile, says a very diplomatic No. Some tourists try to be clever and say they have run out of money. But, even if it's true, he's not going to believe you.

Another thing which often puzzles the rather reserved Westerner is the speedy friendship often encountered here. A good example is the handshake. Moroccans delight in shaking hands at any opportunity. If

4

you bump into your hotel waiter off duty in town, don't be at all surprised if his face lights up with a big smile and he shakes your hand exuberantly. He's not being presumptuous but is usually doing it for two reasons. First, he wants to make you feel at home in his city and secondly, he's proudly showing his friends that he knows nice people, which is complimentary whichever way you look at it.

You might notice that after a Moroccan shakes hands, his right palm brushes his chest. No, your palm isn't sweaty. He's showing that the sincerity of his handshake comes from the heart and it's a charming gesture to copy.

There are several wrinkles you need to get straightened out in order to really enjoy your stay in Tangier. For example, first day tourists often pay over the odds for a taxi. Green taxis, which operate in town only, are not allowed to carry more than three passengers. If you are in a group of four, take a Black taxi. If they get police permission, which does not take long, these can take you outside the Tangier limits but for such trips you are usually better off taking a tourist coach or hiring a car for the day. Young back-packers should take note that public buses are extremely cheap. Inquire at Bradleys, opposite the bus station, which is facing the railway station, if you wish to take a very cheap bus to Tetuan or the Ceuta border post.

For short trips round Tangier, the Green taxis, known as Petit Taxi, are extremely cheap though you might be asked to pay two or three times the correct amount if the meter has not been switched on.

So, if you flag down a cruising taxi, settle the price in advance. This should be done standing on the pavement. The longer you stand there talking, the cheaper the price gets. Don't get in and then start to haggle. This puts you at a psychological disadvantage as the driver knows you are most unlikely to get out.

Haggling over a taxi may seem odd to most Westerners but in Tangier it is not at all unusual. In fact, tourists quickly realise they can bargain for almost anything in this financially democratic city. There's a shrewd joke here which states : "Buy something from me today and tomorrow I could have got it for you much cheaper". Don't be shocked or offended if the first price you are offered seems outlandish. It's all part of the game. Only tourists pay the first price asked.

Some more tips : Ivory on sale in Tangier is sometimes genuine but not if it is suspiciously white. And not those See-nothing, Say-nothing, Hear-nothing monkey necklaces mostly sold by street vendors. They look as though they have been carved from aged tusks or horns but are cunningly disguised plastic.

Silver items look superb but sometimes they are not pure silver but a clever mix. Beware when buying Jade. The odds are that it is the cheap and easily scratched stone known as Bowenite which is exported world wide from places like Hong Kong and Taiwan. The same applies to amber, which has been worn as jewellery since the Stone Age. Many people think amber is a stone but it's actually the fossilised resin from Baltic pine trees and gives off an aromatic pine smell when burnt with the hot point of a needle, which is one sure way of giving a shopkeeper the needle if you want to test whether it's genuine. Plastic, of course, gives off a nasty smell when the hot needle goes in. Fake amber is also made from copal resin which, when rubbed with ether, makes it sticky to touch and touchy shopkeepers go quite faint if you apply this test.

Many an American tourist has happily paid up to 300 dollars for a silver-lined Rif rifle said to be 100 years old, blissfully unaware that it was lovingly manufactured last month and rusted by being hung in water for two weeks. If you haggle really hard that rifle can be yours for less than £30 and even then the shopkeeper will be making a handsome profit.

Leather jackets are beautifully soft but rather buy the better quality because the rain back home, don't ask us why, can make the cheaper ones shrink or the colour run.

When buying bargain brass and copper teapots or kettles, look at the inside carefully. The same goes for those mirrors in gorgeous brass frames. Check the back is also solid brass and not just a thin leaf covering. If it is thin, you have a powerful haggling point. If you want quality make sure the design is engraved because stamped is cheaper gear.

Handwoven rugs are obviously more expensive than machine made because natural fibres are used as well as vegetable dyes. But how can you tell one from the other ? A good clue. The colour runs in the cheaper ones so, if in doubt, ask the seller to wet a corner and rub it hard. If it's genuine he will be pleased to prove it.

If you want an American or British newspaper from one of the youngsters who hawk them round town, check the official price, which should be stamped at the top right hand corner of the front page or in the Stop Press section.

When you walk along the Bvd Pasteur there's a good chance you will meet Diamond Dan. Acting very furtively he will show you a large diamond set in a heavy and hallmarked gold ring. He will whisper that he found it in the lounge of a leading hotel and his starting price is usually about £100. Don't bother. It's a mass-produced Italian fake, even the hallmark on the shank, and he paid less than 20 Dirham for it.

A variation of this lurk is the large gold ring which Robert the Ringer will tell you he found on the beach. Glancing all round as if he fears being seen, Robert will tell you he's two months behind on his rent. Don't fall for it. He may be poorly dressed but that is part of his act and he finds buyers every day. He will show you the gold hallmark and may let you hold the ring for a few seconds so you can feel how heavy it is. Yet whatever he says or does, do not pay the £100 he hopefully demands. Haggle hard and he will part with it for a tenth because the hallmark is a fake and the weight is caused by lead underneath the gold-plated coin bearing the face of Queen Elizabeth, though he will tell you it's Victoria. Also produced in Italy, these rings cost only 50 pence to manufacture.

Many tourists have happily paid 100 times that. Hilariously, a top Scotland Yard man paid £40 for one of those rings while on holiday here last year. He told us it was a present for his father. When told the ring was a fake the cop shrewdly replied : "That did occur to me but it doesn't matter. The ring still looks great and my father's friends won't know the difference". We didn't have the heart to tell him that after being worn for one month the gold dip wears off and the ring turns black.

When buying day trip tickets from smaller travel agencies triple-check all times, dates and other details. We say this because here, we have a language problem with the word Yes. Moroccans have the quaint habit of saying yes in answer to some questions when it should be No. This may sound like the Queen talking to Alice in Wonderland but the reason is that some locals, particularly younger ones, will say Yes whether they understand you or not. This may sound daft but they have a great desire to please tourists and they sometimes think a No answer might sound rude. In other cases they will say Yes because that's what they think you want to hear. Then there's that extra problem created by us when we ask a question such as, "You haven't got a match, have you ?" That makes sense to us but sounds quite negative to someone not fluent in English.

If you suspect this is happening when you ask if the bus leaves at eleven and he says Yes, turn the question round by asking if you can catch the bus at ten. If he says Yes again, you have a problem.

Testing this strange phenomenon, we spoke to a young Moroccan on the beach one bright, sunny day. Pointing to the sky, we said it looked as if it was going to rain. The youngster peered up at the totally cloud-less sky and said Yes. His reasoning, quite sensible to him, was that we were obviously guests in his country and if we were crazy enough to see rain clouds overhead, we clearly wanted it to rain. That being so, he certainly was not going to be rude and say there was something seriously wrong with our eyesight.

This is quite typical of the fabulous diplomacy you will often encounter. We once saw an elderly British couple walking along the seafront Avenue D'Espagne with a 14 year-old unofficial guide. Pointing to one of the tall palm trees, the husband said it was a peanut tree. When his dubious wife turned to the young Moroccan and asked if it really was a peanut tree, he kept a straight face and said it was. No ways was that wise young local going to embarrass the husband in front of his missus by explaining how peanuts really grew.

Another good tip. Don't flash a wallet full of high denomination banknotes. Yes, there are pickpockets here, just as in other big city, although statistically, Tangier is quite innocent when compared with London, where official Scotland Yard estimates indicate that pickpoc-kets rob 100,000 people every year. Don't believe anyone who tells you Tangier is a hotbed of crime or that it is dangerous to walk alone in the Kasbah. Crimes with violence are virtually unknown here. Old ladies do not get mugged in their homes as regularly happens overseas. Child battering and sex crimes are also unheard of in this city.

It can be dangerous for anyone to walk down dark alleys in any city overseas but dozens of tourists walk through Tangier's Kasbah on their own during the day and suffer no problems.

Police investigations disclose the surprising fact that nearly all the tourists who experience trouble in the Kasbah brought it upon them-selves by their rudeness, arrogance or just plain stupidity. These people, who swagger around believing all foreigners are inferior, get exactly what they ask for.

The police in Tangier are extremely efficient. They are very clued up as to what is going on and make every effort to combat all forms of crime. They also help anyone who is polite, particularly visitors, as the

8

Moroccan Government realises just how important tourism is to Tangier's economy. Any well-mannered guest will always be treated like a V.I.P.

This does not mean that Tangier is Paradise on Sea. There are several dodgy characters who try to take tourists for a ride. You already know about Diamond Dan and Robert the Ringer, but we have other Slippery Sams. For instance, if you are not careful you might easily find yourself being short-changed. The trick here is body language. Most Westerners, when being handed change, start to move away, automatically. What they don't realise is that by moving away, even by an inch, they are stopping the rest of the change from coming.

Our short-change artists are true professionals. When you buy something costing, say 25 Dirhams, with a 100 Dirham note, they hand you 70 Dirham change in notes with an air of finality and then turn to speak to someone else as a diversionary tactic. If you stand your ground and look expectant, the short-changer ends his conversation with the other person, fumbles in another pocket and smilingly hands you the other five Dirham, in coins, as if he had intended to give it to you anyway. There's no way you can criticise him because you can't prove he didn't have that intention. But you can smile very broadly and look deep into his eyes, which tells him you are not the mug he first thought.

Another thing to watch is the bill in any restaurant, particularly in Ceuta, as waiters can make mistakes. By mistake of course. Watch for those Continental ones that can look like sevens and fours looking like nines.

The biggest mystery in Tangier is the case of the vanishing centimes. Some items cost, let's say two Dirhams and 70 centimes but tourists often get charged a round three Dirham because shopkeepers adopt the cosy attitude that holidaymakers can't be bothered with all those little gold-coloured five, ten and 20 centime coins.

For easy reckoning, let's regard ten centimes as being one penny. This means the shopkeeper kept three pence. It doesn't seem much when you are on holiday and many tourists don't even notice, particularly when buying a litre bottle of Coca Cola which costs far more back home.   .

During a special investigation, the Rogue's Guide interviewed 50 tourists and found that 38 of them had not handled a gold coloured five, ten or 20 centime coin. As for the silver coloured one centime, even many British and American residents are unaware they exist. This is not surprising when you know there are 100 silver centimes to each Dirham, but they are certainly used by locals in the market places where the price of fruit and veg is usually marked in centimes.

To make this more complicated, the stall holders call them Francs, which is a throwback to the days of the French. But ignore Francs and think in Dirham. If a kilo of oranges is price tagged 300 centimes, you simply divide by 100. Which equals three Dirham. For those who can't divide, just lop off the last two noughts. You still get three. Or you can ask the shopkeeper for the price in Dirham. Good Luck !

Bargaining, the incredible art of

While Tangier tradesmen make every effort to keep prices high, it is sometimes necessary to decrease them at short notice. Two seconds later, to be precise.

The speed at which the second and third price comes down depends entirely on your awareness, your sense of humour, your battle prowess and, most important, your ability to counter-attack with a fast answer.

Don't be surprised if that makes bargaining sound like warfare. It is exactly that. A war of words which the best man will win. Him, not you. If that smacks of being a generalisation to which you take exception because you know you are a good businessman back home, prepare for more annoyance because the cruel truth is that, compared to the Moroccan, you are a babe in arms. It doesn't matter who you are (and that includes us, dear reader) the Moroccan trader will always win. Even if you are that extremely rare tourist who haggles with expertise, you will never get him to part with any item unless he is making a very good profit.

Another thing : When he is finished with you, the Moroccan will always let you walk away believing you strangled a good bargain out of him, leaving him with a pitiful profit. That's a major part of his war game, particularly if you are with your wife. If you are a good adversary, his eyes will give your wife the sad, injured spaniel look to recruit her feminine sympathy - against you. It's quite amazing how often this below-the-belt trick works. The Moroccan, quite rightly, believes the English saying that all's fair in love and war and he will use any weapon to stop you beating him down to the danger point where his basic 100 to 200 per cent profit is threatened.

The fast answer is his usual weapon. Whatever you say to a shop-keeper, he will give you an answer. It's your job to jab back with a quick retort. Fail to do that and you are stuck with the price reached at that stage.

After buying a couple of items in Tangier, most Westerners kid themselves they are really good at bargaining when, in fact, they are kindergarten standard. OK, big shot, so you don't believe it ? Then try selling that item you got so cheaply. Go anywhere in Tangier and try to recover even half the price you paid for it. Then see what happens.

Tangier really can be a very cheap place. But only if you work at it, which means haggling as a reflex. For those people modest enough to admit they are not such hot shots, we offer the following guide lines :

The essence of being a good intelligence agent is visual awareness. If you accept that basic premise, you will quickly realise that every Moroccan trader is a born James Bond. Watch his eyes when they are observing you, or others. It's all lookee, lookee. He misses nothing. You might think he would be foxed if you took off all your expensive jewellery before dealing with him. But that's not so. He does not judge on those things alone. Like a fortune teller, he will notice the absence of hair and the paler skin on the finger normally holding the wedding or engagement ring.

His eyes also assess your teeth to see what condition they are in, which tells him how much or how little you have spent on them and whether or not you smoke. He also notices the condition of your hair, your fingernails and if you have callouses on your palms. Or, in the case of a woman, he looks to see whether the backs of her hands bear tell-tale cracks caused by washing clothes.

He is also a keen student of body language. Rather like a poker player, he looks for signs of shyness, vanity or nervous hand movements, such as instinctively reaching for your wallet when he mentions a lower sounding (to you, not him) price. It only takes him a few seconds to compute all these aspects which, of course, give him a good edge when you start to bargain.

If there's one thing a Moroccan respects, it is an· ingenious and friendly bargainer. For a start, you must never appear keen to buy any item. Adopt a bored look and ask the price as if you are merely window shopping. Whatever price he gives, stifle a yawn or look horrified and start to move away with great determination. That, right at the beginning, may half trick him into half considering that you are not half as daft as he first thought.

His next move will be to call you back with, "OK. Give me a price". This is muttered in such a way that it sounds like a surrender to your shrewdness. But don't be fooled. It's a clever pumping question, aimed at ferreting out what value YOU place on the item. Fall for it and you are doomed. Using his many years of expertise, he will be able to assess your offer and manoeuvre accordingly.

Instead of making him an offer, pick up the item in question and make a long, slow, meticulous examination of it. This is nerve-wracking for any salesman and often shakes his self-confidence because he knows full well it is not worth anything near the first price he demanded. Then give him a below-the-belt punch by ending your examination with a scornful look and putting it down with exaggerated care, as though you fear it will fall to pieces if jolted. Follow this up with a teasing smile and say : "No. You give me a price. It's not really worth bargaining for".

Don't worry, he will understand and, if you are lucky, he will give you a price which, we must emphasise, he will hate doing. If he doesn't, then you know your charade of indifference has not fooled him. Even then all is not lost. Give him a bigger smile, which might frighten him into thinking you know something, and offer him one third of his asking price.

His hands will fly up as though he has been shot through the heart and his face will register shock equivalent to seven points on the Richter scale. He will then almost certainly match your offer with a great show of disappointment. Ignore the disappointment. It's quite definitely a con. The   fact that he has entered into a haggling situation proves quite conclusively that your offer of one third wasn't far wrong. If your offer had been really ridiculous, which means somewhere in the region of his buying in price, he would have turned his back on you in disgust, wouldn't he ? Let's turn this round and look at it from another angle. When you are haggling for a cheap machine-sewn Moroccan garment in cotton, keep in mind that depending on quality, the garment worker probably got between six and nine Dirham for making it. Subtract the cost of the material and the maker's profit and then add about 600 per cent. Now you have a fair idea of the trader's first asking price, often between 80 and 90 Dirham which, if he is strangled really hard, he will reduce to about 50 Dirham. At that price he's still making about 100 per cent profit. Apologists for free enterprise might claim that 100 per cent profit is not really exhorbitant because the 'poor' trader has large overheads to pay and his stock represents substantial capital investment lying idle.

Such misleading reasoning might work overseas, but not here. Shop rents in Tangier are quite low compared to rents elsewhere. Labour costs and electricity are far cheaper here and, in any case, the stock in many bazaars is obtained on credit. No wonder they laughingly say it is so quiet in Tangier after midnight that the only sound heard is the rustle of banknotes being counted by tourist bazaar owners.

Another humourous thing about Tangier shopkeepers is that many of them understand English but pretend they don't. This gives them a tremendous advantage during bargaining sessions as it reduces your verbal potential. And, of course, every time you say something in an aside to your wife during the haggling, you are providing the shopkeeper with vitally important ammunition quite apart from what your wife may reveal in reply.

Women tourists look more carefully at a garment and, noticing all the intricate stitching and hard work that has been put into it, feel rather guilty. In their mind's eye they see some little seamstress doing all that work in a back room, and compare it with the price husband is trying not to pay. Invariably, the wife will turn to hubby and say : "Go on. Pay the price being asked. It's worth it". This female reasoning, though commendably compassionate, is quite nonsensical. The price her husband pays the shopkeeper makes not a scrap of difference to the wage given to the seamstress.

Another typical slice of misleading reasoning is the argument that

"We pay what we think it is worth". But how can tourists, here for a short holiday, really know the true value of any local product. The only assessment they can normally make is based on prices back home, related to their cost of living and their wages, which simply do not compare easily with Tangier.

Back now to bargaining. Another good thing to know is the "last price" routine. When a Moroccan says these words it usually means that's as low as he will go. But it can also be a psychological ploy to make you feel insecure or to give the impression that he is losing patience with your obvious meanness. This is where your sense of humour is essential. If you frown and continue to haggle seriously, you risk him losing face if others are listening, which they usually are, and he may break off all negotiations in annoyance at your crude technique.

But crack a joke, preferably one that flatters him, and you might find that the last price wasn't because you have given him an honourable way of reducing it.

What kind of joke can you crack ? Well, let's say you are haggling for a pair of those flip-flop slippers, known here as babouches. He asks 40 Dirham and you ruthlessly offer 15. He comes back with 30 and you up it to 20, adding that this is your last price. He will probably tell you that 25 is his last price because he paid 20 Dirham for the slippers and is therefore making only a meagre five profit. Neither of you wants to lose face over that five Dirham and it would appear that a stalemate has been reached.

Not so. Now's the time for that flattering joke. Lean forward close to his face and peer intently into his eyes for about ten seconds. Then draw back, slowly shake your head with a big, theatrical smile and say, in a loud voice : "No. I can't believe you are only making five Dirham profit. Your eyes give you away. They are far too clever for that".

Even if he genuinely doesn't comprehend English completely, you can be sure he will understand the mood. And if he doesn't, some Moroccan bystander will and he'll translate your joke quickly to much laughter from all present. Do it right and it's even money you'll get those slippers for 20 Dirham.

Mind you, Moroccans have a fabulous sense of humour and you can easily come unstuck if he tops your joke with a better one. In which case, you must be a good loser, shake hands and pay the man his price.

Good Buys to Your Money

The travel agent who advised you to "spend" your holiday in Tangier probably used that word with tongue in cheek as there is an old joke in this city which suggests tourists bring half their holiday clothes but double their money. Tangier is so full of bargains that some people have to buy an extra suitcase to cart all their goodies away.

You will have little difficulty finding your own bargains but the Rogue's Guide offers the following snippets which may prove time and money saving.

The word Morocco is synonymous with fine leather. So much so that Bing Crosby and Bob Hope, in their film "Road to Morocco", sang that, like Webster's Dictionary, they were Morocco bound. Local leather is not only a good buy but long-lasting. You will find many shops and bazaars selling suitcases, handbags, wallets and jewel cases but don't forget you can have superb shoes made by hand and to your own design.

Should you need urgent clothing repairs done by hand, quickly and cheaply, visit Abdelhak Younoussi at his tiny shop at 3 Siaghins, next door to the Ray Charly hamburger joint in the Petit Socco (Small Market). He even repairs torn trousers or a broken zipper and you can wear one of his djellabahs while you wait.

For first day tourists perhaps we should explain that a djellabah, often striped, is the garment with a hood and it is worn by men and women. A Caftan is a cassock like dress worn by women and is often heavily embroidered round the neck. A Kandura looks something like a coloured nightshirt and is worn by men. Don't be shy, Bert, you won't look poofy. And it's amazingly cool to wear at home on a hot day.

You will have no trouble finding these traditional Moroccan garments. Tangier shops are full of them. If you want something rather different though, try the high fashion Moroccan garments with a contemporary European style at Volubilis Boutique run by American-born Karla opposite Romero's Spanish restaurant in Rue Prince Moulay Abdellah. Her husband Mohamed, who is also a talented artist, runs the other Volubilis in the Petit Socco.

Right next door to Karla's boutique in town there's Sportswear Mode run by San Francisco-born Margaret which offers the latest New York and Paris style swimwear and beach clothing. Margaret is usually there between 11am and 1pm.

A good tip for women buying local garments is for them to get matching braids or cottons in case repairs are needed years later.

The same applies to matching zip fasteners which, at prices starting from about thirteen pence, are amazingly cheap. For all these items, walk down the Rue de Italy from the Grand Socco. On the right hand side you will find several haberdashery shops with bargains cheaper than in town. We recommend numbers 42 and 48 and also 16 Rue Sebou just round the corner.

Most women like looking at jewellery, so no female visit to Tangier would be complete without a walk along Rue Touahin. To find it, walk down Rue Semmarin from the Grand Socco and it's the first street, street not archway, on the right. Known as the Street of Gold, it has 44 small jewellery shops crammed with silver rings, brooches and medallions of all kinds. You pay slightly more for gold here and remember it bears no hallmark.

Also to be seen in most shops are the Hand of Fatima good luck charms. The hand usually has two thumbs. Another unusual item is the eight-tier seed pearl necklace sewn on to a fabric neck strap. Costing from about £20, these look so regal that crafty countesses wear them with their evening gowns back home. And so do some dolly birds.

Talking of dolls, unique ones are sold by **Madame Diane Lahlou** who runs a pretty china shop at 54 Bvd Pasteur next to the Avis hire car office. All wearing various national costumes, they have hand-painted porcelain faces and cost between £10 and £35. Another lovable doll is the Anna Poupee washable rag doll sold by Pamtex from a display cabinet in the Hotel Rif foyer and also from the cute shop run by Fatima on the mezzanine floor of the Hotel Minzah.

Another good bargain is the Samovar, known here as a Babor. They are stunning in brass or copper, the smaller ones costing anything from 200 Dirham, the more spectacular ones about 2000. Incidentally, tourists from Germany, France and Spain are buying Samovars not only as ornaments but also as containers for sherry, punch and even home-made beer at parties.

Some tourists who do not like haggling wait until they have been in Tangier three or four days before going shopping. This is not a bad idea as it gives them time to acquire a better awareness of local values, which is not at all easy particularly if they are staying at a four or five star hotel.

For tourists who hate haggling but can't wait to shop, we suggest the Ensemble Artisanal art school on the left hand side of Rue Belgique, just up from the Cafe de Paris. Here you can watch masters and their students at work and buy a wide range of goods at fixed prices.

Several no-haggling, fixed price shops are to be found along the Boulevard Pasteur and along the sea front. At these shops and bazaars every item usually has a price tag. Look at the copper, brass, silver or pewter tea pots costing from 35 Dirham up. They have unique designs making them a great conversation piece when you have the neighbours in for tea back home, Mabel.

One speciality we love is the little brass crab, spider and tortoise ornaments which are cunning ashtrays. Priced from 20 to 35 Dirham, these make unique and cheap presents.

If you're looking for promotion, Bert, get the boss one of those lovely copper and brass kettles in the olde worlde British style, from 80 Dirham upwards. These are not the antiques they look but your boss won't know the difference. The same applies to the pirate style pistols priced from 45 Dirham which, although they were made yesterday, look like real antiques.

If you buy several things in fixed price shops, and ask for it, they will probably give you a special discount. In fact, we suggest you visit several fixed price shops, compare all the prices and then decide for yourself which gives the best bargains. But do keep in mind that in bazaars where prices are normally tagged, you will sometimes find articles which are not. These could be catch lines, which is another reason we urge you to compare prices before buying.

Tourists who have no French are often confused by signs reading "Solde" in shop windows. It does not mean the shop or the items in the window have been sold. The word is French for sale bargain.

If you go to the Fondouk Market, just down the 43 steps past the El Minzah Hotel, you can see a wide range of cheap pottery.

One item making an unusual present for kids is the clay piggy bank costing three to eight Dirham depending on quality or pattern. It's fun as it has a slot for the money to go in but no hole at the bottom for it to be taken out. When kids want money for sweets they think twice before breaking the bank.

Also good for pottery is Ahmed Oughar's little shop at 41 Rue Salah Eddine el Ayoubi, the street leading down to the Port from the Grand Socco. Opposite the pottery shop, through the archway alóngside number 90, is the Clothing Market but if you want those striped Berber blankets and shawls, visit the Ladies Market just across from the English church of St Andrews.

If you want a T-shirt, don't miss the Hollywood Shop run by American-born Margaret and her husband Amal in the arcade next to the Algemene Bank at 48 Bvd Pasteur. The couple specialise in custom designed T-shirts bearing trendy motifs or any slogan of your choice. Also offering T-shirts with slogans is Arrouah at 25 Avenue Mohammed Five, just up from the Post Office.

If you are interested in good clothing for the younger child, try the little shop run by Ruby Assayag at 19 Ave. Mohammed Five. It's next door to the Atlas pavement cafe. Most days you will see men of all ages sitting inside the Atlas Cafe, throwing dice on to a glass-topped board. Americans know the game. It's Parchesi. The British don't know the name because a shrewd Londoner came here years ago, saw Parchesi and liked it. But he thought it was too complicated for British brains, so he simplified the rules and made a fortune by introducing it to the United Kingdom as Ludo. Was he right to simplify the rules ? Find out for yourself by buying a Parchesi board from the tiny brass shop on the 43 steps just past the the El Minzah Hotel.

And, as a special service to our readers we give you, for free, gratis and for nothing, with no hidden surcharge, this century only, never to be repeated, the rules of the game, translated into English, from the Chinese, at enormous cost, at the end of this book. Hey, Dad, there's something fishy here. The people who wrote this book are giving something away for nothing. Yes, son, but the trick there is that they probably own that shop on the 43 steps. (Author's note : Not so Dad. We don't).

If the above nonsense gave you a headache, get some pain killers from the chemist. All chemist chops in Tangier are good but our favourites are the Pharmacy Centrale, opposite the Official Tourist Office in Blvd Pasteur, the Pharmacy Pasteur next door to the Cafe de Paris and the Pharmacy Paris opposite where the English-speaking French owner gives free advice. Good buys are vitamin pills and you will need lotion for mosquito bites if you sleep in your bedroom with the lights on and windows open at night during the summer.

Quite a few visitors to Tangier suffer from Prickly Heat on legs, arms and chest, not realising it is caused by failing to soap their bodies properly in warm water after using sun tan oil all day. A cold shower does not remove the oil properly and the pores remain blocked. The skin complains by erupting in itchy lumps. The chemist usually prescribes anti-histamine tablets and a good, hot and soapy bath.

Not often found in chemists but seen in the market, is loose henna for colouring hair. But women over 40 should not dye their hair because there's a wise old Moroccan saying which states that only the young dye good. One unusual local item is good for the hair though. This is Ghasool, pronounced rhasool. It looks like chunks of brown mud and you can buy it in half kilo lots for a couple of Dirham. Placed in hot water, a small amount dissolves quickly and makes a great shampoo and conditioner all in one. Also good for the scalp. This is perhaps where the saying 'She's got rocks in her head' comes from.

A different kind of rock is Shib, a white and almost transparent crystal costing about 5 Dirham a kilo. At home, break it into about 100 small pieces and give one to every male friend as a present. Dab it on your face if you cut yourself when shaving, Bert. Far superior to the expensive styptic pencils you buy in the West because each piece lasts about three years. Women can also use it they cut their legs while shaving.

Another popular present to take home are the locally made brass or silver bangles. Some cost as little as 10 Dirham each and you can find them in the window of the Indian shop alongside the Cafe de Paris and then walk to other nearby shops to check price and quality to suit your taste and pocket.

Nearly all women like perfume and that being so, there's a little shop they should know about. It's in the Medina and not easy to find so we give you two directions. Take a taxi to Rue de Italy then ask anyone to direct you to Perfumerie Madini at 14 Rue Sebou. Alternatively, get yourself to the Petit Socco and there, in the square, you will see a narrow alley between the Cafe Tingis and the Cafe Centrale. The latter cafe, by the way, was the favourite meeting place of many world famous writers and artists during the Fifties and Sixties.

Walk down that narrow alley, passing dozens of fascinating bazaars until it becomes Rue Sebou. Madini's perfume shop is on the left. If you reach a little square with women selling bread in the centre of it, you have walked about thirty paces too far. Retrace your steps and you should see Madini's place on your right, next to a haberdashery shop.

Mr Madini has 70 varieties of very good perfume, including all the famous brands such as Dior, Carven, Givenchy, Yves Saint Laurent and so on. You might say Madini sells copies but one thing to keep in mind is that he's a world expert whose perfumes hold you smell bound. His family has been making perfume for 14 generations, which rather makes Jean Patou and Coco Chanel look like beginners. Forget about those highly taxed French scents you pay through the nose for and which contain at least 50 per cent alcohol and distilled water. This man sells the pure oil and it's cheaper than the stuff you can get back home.

Take your own perfume there and test it against his brand in the same name if you wish to be surprised. Look at his Musk in solid or liquid form and Mr Madini will tell you it is from the throat glands of the gazelle. But he's just being polite. Musk comes from the gazelle alright, but not its throat. As you stand in this shop you will notice that it is popular with Moroccan women, which confirms you are getting good quality.

Mr Madini, who speaks English, also sells Eau de Cologne of super refinement and he keeps it up on the top shelf in large fancy bottles.

Watch as he mixes five or six different brands for the local ladies who adore Miss Dior mixed with Estee Lauder and others into a bombshell of an aroma. Madini's perfumery is closed between Ipm and 4pm and all day on Friday. If you are a fast-moving American tourist who misses Mr Madini, don't worry. You can buy his perfumes from Talisman, a smart shop run by two delightful Tangier veterans, Dulcie and William Roppenecker at 68 Tinker Street, Woodstock, New York.

Other good buys to consider in Tangier are Saffron and the local Olive Oil. You can get a cheap litre tin of olive oil which would cost at least three times more overseas, but gourmets prefer the litre tin costing between 20 and 25 Dirham because the cheaper variety is a second or third pressing of the olive and tends to have a slightly bitter taste. Saffron, at about 4 Dirham for a small envelope, is a good bargain if you get the red thread, not the powder. For male readers who don't cook maybe we should add that saffron is the stuff used to tint rice yellow.

Enjoy a stroll through the Covered Market. To get there, walk down Rue Semmarin from the Grand Socco and turn into the first archway on your right. There, just past the four ladies squatting on the floor selling eggs, you will find a motley collection of shops. Say hello to the Haji (Haj) who sells tasty pancake shaped bread. A Haji is a Muslim who has made a pilgrimage to Mecca.

If you wish to taste the sophistication of the rich in Tangier, visit Maison de Velasco, the chic antique shop run by the superb decorator Adolfo Velasco. It's across the road just up from the post office. Two other antique shops are the Chez Mansour at 78 Rue de la Liberte, opposite the El Minzah and the Gallery Tindouf two doors below. Further down is the Bazaar Tindouf, full of junky delights and bargains.

A difficult antique shop to find is Mohamed Ouazzani's place at 9 Rue Synagogue, a street on the right as you walk down Rue Semmarin from the Grand Socco. No kids are allowed in this shop as the owner has over one million dollars worth of stock all over the floor and hanging from the ceiling.

If you wish to see what must be the smallest and cheapest shops in the world, go to Hong Kong Alley. To get there go down those 43 stone steps past the El Minzah Hotel. At the bottom, look across to your left and the group of fruit stalls. Walk through them and on your left you will see two or three small foundries making hand-wrought iron railings etc. This is where Hong Kong Alley starts.

One clever young stallholder is Youness Mbarek, aged 27, who specialises in repairing spectacles. He has hundreds of old pairs and can match almost any frame or replace that tiny screw or hinge.

Another man sells secondhand false teeth. Goodness knows where he gets them but if the cap fits, wear it, kind of thing.

Quite apart from the novelty value, Hong Kong Alley is a must for tourists who are shopkeepers back home. They will feel like millionaires when they see the stock on some tiny stalls and compare it with theirs. Americans who have been in Neiman Marcus, that ritzy Dallas, Texas store which sells such items as his and hers midget submarines (that's not a joke) will also be able to make some fascinating comparisons.

Some of the stalls in Hong Kong Alley are not even stalls in actual fact, but simply a man sitting on the floor surrounded by a wide variety of items such as bits of old iron, rusty nuts, bolts, screws, locks, keys, radio parts, books, lamps and broken electrical plugs and empty bottles of all types.

Yes, these stalls sell anything under the sun which might possibly be used again. A good example of this are those disposable plastic cigarette lighters that most Westerners throw away when empty. Believe it or not, these empty lighters are on sale in Hong Kong Alley for two or three pence. Try and guess why before you read the next sentence. The flint in the empty lighter still works and gives off a spark which is used to light a gas cooker.

While on the subject of these cigarette lighters, if you have one that needs filling or is faulty, go and see Mustapha Belhajrouas, aged 27, in his little grocery shop at 86 Rue Emsallah. If possible, go there between II and noon. As a sideline, Mustapha repairs all kinds of lighters, even those expensive electronic ones. He also sells old lighters of all kinds at reasonable prices. This bright young man is a real magician with lighters and is known in Tangier as the King of them. He has discovered a way of filling those throwaway ones and will do it for one Dirham.

It will fascinate you to watch this nimble-fingered chap take a lighter to pieces in a matter of seconds. He's completely self-taught. His interest in lighters started when he was aged eight and took one to bits for fun. But the most extraordinary aspect is that Mustapha does all his work with one hand. He was born with only one.

To get to Mustapha's shop, walk along the Rue Mexique, going away from town until you reach the Lux Cinema. There, on your left is Rue Emsallah. It's terrific for cheap bargains and the only place in Tangier's new town which closely resembles the Kasbah in terms of shopping and visual entertainment.

If you are a junk addict, don't miss the Flea Market in the Grand Socco. Stand at the black taxi rank and you will see a small white concrete office. This is the Police Poste for Taxis and bears a sign to that effect. Right behind this office, as you face the pretty mosque, there's a tiny alley between shops selling TV and radio sets. This is the entrance to the Flea Market. Although small, it is packed with stalls selling almost everything. It has several small coffee places, barbers shops and even a stall for coin collectors and old camera enthusiasts. Just below the Flea Market is a long street known as the Juteah which is also lined with dozens of stalls selling all kinds of junk.

For higher class junk and antiques, walk up Rue Belgique from the Cafe de Paris, turn left into Rue Holland and walk along until you come to Furniture Row which is on the right hand side. Don't miss number 24, which looks like a private house on the left, but is actually a three-storied secondhand shop.

Just past this house, on the left, you will see the square-shaped Fez Market with stalls selling everything from groceries to tropical birds and is popular with many British and American locals.

If you wish to see the local weavers in action then go back to those well-worn 43 stone steps just past the El Minzah. About 60 paces from the bottom of the steps, on your right, you will find an archway leading into the Fondouk Market Square which is crammed with fruit and veg stalls. As you enter you will see a cobbler working at his little bench. Next to him is a man who specialises in repairing metal teapots, kettles and ventilation pipes. In the right hand corner of the Fondouk a flight of stairs goes up to the weavers section. Watch these industrious people spinning superb blankets and cloth on hand-operated looms over 100 years old and their children helping by spinning wool and cotton on old bicycle wheels.

If its a pretty handmade and high quality rug you want at a reasonable price, go and introduce yourself to English-born Brenda in her shop at 46 Rue el Mansour Dahabi, just along from the Roxy Cinema which is in the street opposite the main Post Office. Brenda is usually there at noon and is well worth meeting as she knows just about all the British residents in Tangier.

If you are a keen cameraman, keep one or two Dirham coins ready as you walk round Tangier as you will surely need them. Some Berber women resent being photographed and in any case, it's a matter of politeness to ask for permission or even offer to pay first. Yorkshire farm workers or London dustbin men could easily get annoyed if a rich American tourist rushed up and started banging off shots of them in their working clothes.

One man who doesn't mind cameras is the camel operator on the beach. He knows tourists love having pictures taken riding a camel. But negotiate the price first or you might be charged for every click of your shutter. Another man who clicks with cameras, whether you want to buy or sell, is bearded Mohamed Holte, a rotund chap who walks through town with four or five good quality cameras hanging round his chest. If he doesn't have what you want he will escort you to Boutique Everything at 3 Rue des Chretiens, that narrow street alongside the Cafe Tingis in the Petit Socco. There, they have a window full of secondhand cameras and lenses at various prices.

While on the beach you will probably meet another rotund fellow. This is Charlie Brown, who calls all British tourists Charlie Brown, Charlie Chaplin or just plain Charlie if you buy from him without haggling.

He has an arch sense of humour and will offer to swop his wife for yours which might seem a compliment, depending on what your wife looks like, but is just part of his buttering up technique. He always carries a large bundle of garments with tourist trinkets dangling from his wrists for which he laughingly asks a tourist price.

If you are bald, Charlie Brown takes off his knitted skull cap and shouts snap. Yes, he's a laugh a minute but watch out if he asks whether you have been to Tunisia. This is a clever pumping question used by many salesmen in Tangier. The idea is to find out if you have experienced Middle East type haggling techniques. If you haven't, the price goes up. So say you have been there. Charlie Brown cracks every joke in the book to keep his prices high but if you haggle with humour you get a fair bargain in the end because Charlie Brown is a good sport. Don't ignore him totally because his selling patter is highly entertaining as well as educational on a shrewdness level.

Willie the Wallet is another beach character who might offer you a pretty leather wallet for two Dirham which gains your attention. Pay attention.

Others characters you might meet are the Furtive Freds who offer a kilo of grass. This is one item in Tangier you should never buy. It's not a good buy but goodbye to your freedom because the local police and customs officials are super efficient and well informed.

Music & Other Fiddles

The catchiest musical ruse in Tangier which will delight teenage tourists, is the tape game. In Britain, America and many parts of Europe, youngsters don't believe in records any more because apart from warping and scratching easily, they are expensive. So they tape the latest pop music at home from radio programmes.

Tangier youngsters go one better. They take their blank tape cassettes to the local record shop, pay about 10 Dirham, and the assistant, using the latest equipment, makes an excellent recording of the latest Rolling Stones and other hit LP's for them.

Both sides are happy. The customer gets a real bargain and the shop makes a tidy profit, particularly if it makes 50 tapes from one LP. The multi-million dollar recording companies overseas are fully aware of this piracy but there's little they can do about it. If British and American shopkeepers did such a thing they could easily be disciplined by threats of legal action for contravention of copyright. The Rogue's Guide is not suggesting tourists should take advantage of such roguish recordings. Goodness gracious, those big recording companies certainly would not approve.

Many things are not what they appear to be in Tangier. "Hadey" the best belly dancer in town is a good example. While enjoying a Moroccan Evening at top class hotels such as the Tanjah Flandria or the Chellah, many male tourists will ogle at the way she swivels her hips seductively and gives them sexy glances. Jealous wives shouldn't worry because Hadey is no lady. He's Abdel Drires, aged 19, and his long black hair is a wig. This lithe young lad is so talented that he teaches the young female belly dancers their trade. So, if a sexy belly dancer runs her fingers through your hair Bert, look closely at the second finger on her right hand. If it has a small scar that has stopped the fingernail growing, that's Abdel. He trapped it in a door when a toddler.

A less amusing kind of musical fiddle in Tangier is the primitive banjo made from a tortoise shell. A few years ago the countryside was full of these harmless and easily tamed creatures. Driving along the roads near the Diplomatic Forest you would see several of them toddling along the tarmac. Today you will be lucky to see one. Sadly, they are caught so that their shells can be turned into banjo's. The worst aspect of this is that musically, the banjo's are useless. But tourists love them because they are cheap novelty souvenirs.

If you want a genuine Moroccan banjo, balalaika or mandoline, whether new or secondhand, visit the Tindouf Bazaar opposite the El Minzah Hotel. This is a fascinating shop crammed full to the ceiling with antiques and junk of every description. Many items are price tagged.   In the main square of the Kasbah, next to the Old Sultan's Palace and the Museum, a musical group often plays tambourines and flute. With them will be a snake charmer who, for a tip, puts a cobra round your wife's neck so that you can take an amusing photograph. Don't worry Bert, Mabel's tongue probably contains more venom because the snake's poison sac has usually been cut out or emptied.

Another enterprising local with a musical touch is the knife sharpener who plays an eleven note Pan flute as he trundles round town pushing a small cart bearing a foot-pedalled grindstone. He also sharpens scissors.

On the beach during the summer season you might hear the sharper sound of a police whistle which is blown when anyone walks across the sand towards the sea fully dressed. Swimmers are expected to undress in the private changing cabins provided by most beach establishments. This is for modesty and security reasons.

Be alert when visiting some of the smaller, side street discos. The man at the door is usually only a doorman and definitely should not charge an entrance fee. Inside, it is wise to ask how much a drink costs before you order it and, if you then decide to buy a drink, pay for it at once. Do not run up a bar bill. Always have plenty of small change and 10 Dirham notes so that you can pay the exact amount there and then. In fact, that's a good rule to apply anywhere in this city.

If you like crowded discos you might find that the bigger hotels give good value. Highly recommended are the discos at the Chellah, the Tanjah Flandria, the Solazur and the Sheherazade. For a panoramic and romantic view of Tangier by night, the flying saucer shaped disco on the top floor of the seafront Almohades Hotel takes some beating. That does not mean you should ignore the other discos. A new one which is becoming popular is the Regine Club just opposite the Roxy Cinema in Rue el Mansour Dahbi.

Another disco with a distinctive character is Scotts in Rue Moutanabi. Started by an Irishman, this place enjoys a friendly trade which cruises in late at night and there's certainly no shortage of young, good looking bachelors as dancing partners. Here, in this tastefully furnished and efficiently run bar, you have a chance to see some of the earlier work by the talented artist, Stuart Church.

They say that every picture is worth a thousand words. Round the walls of Scotts you will see 18 framed pictures of handsome soldiers and pretty drummer boys wearing kilts. The only female face hanging on the wall is that of the British Queen.

One sound often puzzling to first day tourists in Tangier is a man chanting melodiously. This is the Muezzin who, through a loudspeaker system installed in the tower of a mosque, is proclaiming the hours of prayer. His first call to the Faithful is at daybreak. Very few Westerners know what he is singing so here are the words :

"God is most great. I testify that there is no God but Allah. I testify that Mohammed is His Prophet. Come to prayer, come to security. God is great".

For the first call at daybreak, the Muezzin wisely adds the words : 'Prayer is better than sleep'.

Come to the Kasbah

If any man suffers unfair criticism in Tangier it is the official guide. Within hours of arriving in this city you will surely be told that the guide is a lazy, uneducated good for nothing or, alternatively, he is a super slick operator who spends most of his time earning a fortune out of gullible tourists.

This simply is not so. The whole subject of guides is surrounded with half-truths, distortions and deliberately mounted propaganda. The problem almost certainly stems from the strange fact that although many professional writers have written about Tangier, not one of them bothered to interview the guides themselves.

The Rogue's Guide has conducted a special investigation into the subject by interviewing not only Government officials but also the Association of Guides itself. Here are the facts :

Basically, there are two kinds of guide in Tangier. The unofficial and the official. The unofficial guide will approach you in the street with a thousand and one reasons why he should escort you to the Kasbah. One ploy is that he's a student who wishes to practice his English and in a few cases this might well be true. Another method is for him to say he works in the hotel you are staying at. Yet another gambit is for him to say he can arrange good deals for you at his uncle's shop or his cousin's father's great grandmother's shop. What he's hoping for, of course, is that he will earn a commission by taking you to a bazaar where he has a private deal going. If he is related to someone at the shop then it's even money that your father's mother was a Chinaman.

This does not mean that all unofficial guides are a waste of time. Some of the youngsters offering a tour of the Kasbah will be polite, useful and entertaining. But some may not. The choice is yours, but do keep in mind that the Official Tourist Office will not accept responsibility for any resulting problems.

On the other hand, if you hire the services of an official guide you are fully covered. He carries an official green or red badge which bears his guide number.

This number is your insurance against unhappiness because the guide knows full well that if you make a note of that number and submit a complaint against him, an official investigation will be mounted and if your complaint is valid he loses his licence to operate.

Very few people realise the extreme lengths the Moroccan Government goes to in an attempt to ensure that all tourists get a fair deal from official guides. A guide must attend a special training school every day for four years. He must be able to speak fluent Arabic and at least three other languages. After his four years of schooling he must pass a stiff oral and written examination before he is given an official guide badge. There are two training schools for guides, one in Tangier and the other in Rabat. Here, the trainee must learn all aspects of local history, geography, politics and diplomacy. In addition he must acquire an in-depth knowledge of Morocco's imports and exports in case the tourist is a businessman who wants accurate facts and figures.

If you want an official guide you can apply in person at the Official Tourist Office at 29 Boulevard Pasteur. It only takes two or three minutes. Alternatively, you can call in at the Association of Guides, which is above Le Claridge in Blvd Pasteur, or phone direct at 31372. Most of the officials there speak English and they will tell you without delay, which guide is available and which man best suits your requirements.

The cost of hiring an official guide is quite cheap. At the time of writing a guide will give you a full day tour of Tangier for 50 Dirham. If you pay 5 Dirham extra you get the services of a National Guide who carries the coveted red badge. He is not only fully versed on Tangier but the whole of Morocco in case you want accurate information on principal cities such as Casablanca, Fez and Agadir. If you want a National Guide to accompany you to other cities the charge is 100 Dirham daily plus his bed and breakfast costs and two other meals a day.

You do not need to pay any official guide in advance. He gets his money only when you terminate his services. The tip you give depends entirely on whether he has pleased you. If he hasn't, you pay only his hiring fee. Not a penny more.

The most common rumour about official guides is that they retire rich. Everyone in Tangier has heard about the guide who has a fortune in the bank and is building a luxury villa for his retirement. The suggestion here is that guides make a fortune at your expense by taking you to bazaars where they get a percentage of everything you spend. This is only half true. The guides do get a percentage quite often but not at your expense. It makes not a scrap of difference whether you take an official guide with you or not. If there's no guide with you the shopkeeper pockets it for himself. If that sounds odd, the Association of Guides say they are willing to prove it to any Doubting Thomas.

There is another aspect of shopping which is not widely known. Tourists are actually safer with an official guide because some bazaars overcharge unescorted tourists quite ruthlessly. They cannot do this when an official guide is present because if the tourist later complains of being overcharged, the guide gets into trouble with the Tourist Office for allowing it to happen. It is common sense then that the official guide protects his back, and his job, by ensuring you are not fleeced in his presence.

Official guides are not as well off as is generally believed. They have no social security and get no pension. Their actual working period exists for less than five months which is the summer tourist season. For the other seven months they are mostly out of work. The majority of package tourists do not bother to use guides but for those who do there are 115 official guides in Tangier and they are given their assignments on a rota basis. Some can go for three days without getting a client. The fact that official guides do their job properly is clearly proven by the large number of letters and postcards they receive from satisfied tourists all over the world.

Alms for Allah's Sake

Yes, Tangier has beggars, but they are not victimised by the police. In this respect the Moroccan authorities are to be praised for their honesty. They do not hypocritically sweep the beggars into police cells to keep them out of sight when VIP's are in town, as is done in many Western cities.

The official attitude towards beggars in Morocco comes from The Koran which teaches that those enjoying a prosperous or comfortable life should show compassion to the poor and needy. The Giving of Alms is one of the Five Pillars of Islam and constantly reminds the Giver that all men are equal. This Giving is widely practised but particularly at the time of the Prophet Mohammed's Birthday and at New Year, when many rich businessmen who are True Believers give a percentage of their yearly profits to charity.

In most cases the beggars sit quietly in the street waiting for Allah to show his goodness through your sympathy. As you can clearly see, many are genuine have-nots who have lost limbs, were born deformed or have been blinded by disease. If you are in any doubt however, watch from a discreet distance to see if Moroccans drop a coin into his palm. This is a good yardstick as the locals know the genuine beggars.

What should you give ? To most tourists this is a problem because you often cannot judge who deserves what and in any case it simply is not possible to dish out money to every beggar you see. As a general rule never give silver coins. Instead, keep all your gold coloured centimes in a separate pocket and whenever you see a beggar, drop one or two into his hand. It's costing you only a penny or two at a time and you are, in this way, spreading your money in the most sensible way. A British beggar might spit in your face if you gave him one penny, but no Moroccan beggar will ever complain about the smallness of the donation. On the contrary, if he is genuine, he will accept it for what it is. A gift from Allah. And that is never to be scorned.

Lookee Lookee, Cafe Society

As you have surely noticed, the most popular pastime in Tangier is to sit at a pavement cafe and watch our fascinating world go by. There are many to choose from but the best known is the Cafe de Paris at the beginning of Boulevard Pasteur where, if you sit long enough, someone will eventually start up a friendly conversation.

It is most entertaining to sit and watch the endless variety of humans walking past. It's really amazing what you will notice if you concentrate and take mental photographs of every passerby.

Watch the elegant Indian ladies with swishing silk saris and Hindu caste marks ; the Englishmen, conservative, aloof, or condescending, according to caste, or should that be taste ? The languid Frenchmen ; stern-faced and efficient Germans ; Serious Spaniards ; smiling but shrewd Americans ; voluble handshaking Moroccans with their wives wearing modesty veils ; beggars of all types ; bootblacks of all sizes ; lottery ticket salesmen of many numbers, some of them lucky ones ; peanut vendors ; carpet, blanket and garment sellers ; schools of young children all lugging satchels ; shoals of merchant seamen ashore to whoop it up for one night. Tourists of all types, the women hanging on the arms of their men and the men with expensive cameras round their necks , constantly patting their back pockets to see whether their wallets are still there.

Look ! There's a chap with the words PILE WONDER printed on the back of his overalls. No, he's not selling one of those creams guaranteeing relief from discomfort. He's one of several locals who work for a company selling excellent radio and other batteries.

See those dignified Berber women with tattooed chins and hands striding past in traditional handwoven towel-type skirts striped in different colours and huge straw hats with brims so wide they have four woollen suspension tassles attached to the crown.

These hardworking country folk are the indigenous people of Morocco. In the old days they were basically nomadic but today farm industriously, as can be seen from the huge packs of vegetables they and their donkeys carry into town every morning.

If you look closely you will see the Berbers often have a brownish red stain on their hands and feet. The main reason for this is that the Prophet Mohammed dyed his beard red with a paste made from henna leaves and many locals continue to use henna for their hands and feet in emulation of the great man. Some Berber men henna their beards red but not their hair. A secondary reason for using henna on the hands is that it strengthens the skin.

There's never a dull moment sitting outside the Cafe de P. If you don't use all the lumps of sugar with your coffee or tea some smiling little sweet-toothed scamp passing by might ask you for it. If you are shy but want people to talk to you, leave your cigarettes lying on the table in front of you. That's an open invitation which will most likely be taken up by someone wanting a cigarette or a match as an excuse to strike up a conversation.

Just before sundown a completely new flock of gossippers descends on the Cafe de P when hundreds of sparrows invade the evergreen trees along the pavement edge and start chattering about the events of their day before settling down to sleep. Nobody knows why they choose to roost in the town centre every night. Unlike cheeky British sparrows, they never swoop down to the tables for crumbs.

One thing not crummy in the Cafe de Paris complex is the brand new (July 1986) Cœur de Tanger restaurant on the first floor. The entrance, by the way, is in the side street round the corner. It's a super posh place fit for a King (or Queen) and, being expensive (approx 10 quid a head) it's mainly frequented by the local monied class.

If you want to see some of the local characters, try sitting at one of the pavement tables outside the Cafe de P. The Tangier British Polo and Croquet Association is virtually extinct these days and the Over-Eighties American Nudists Leap Frog Team naturally keeps a rather low profile, but there are other fascinating faces.

Caffeine Colin, also known as Coffee Dregs Colin, is a short, slim man with crew cut hair who wears old trousers with an open-necked white shirt. He haunts the Cafe de P and several pavement cafes nearby. If someone has finished their coffee he points at it politely and, when given the nod, gulps the dregs down quickly. Then he wipes his mouth on his shirt sleeve and runs away laughing as the waiters give chase.

Seashell Sam is a tallish, handsome chap in his forties who sells prettily painted seashells and his chat up ploy is to say you or your wife remind him of some famous film star. Reeling off such names as Charles Bronson, Clark Gable, Jane Fonda or Betty Grable, he's a laugh a minute and many tourist couples fall for this flattering gambit, even when they actually resemble Laurel and Hardy.

Foghorn Fred can often be seen outside the Cafe de Paris. He shouts in a distinctive megaphone voice and carries a swagger stick under his arm and sometimes waves it at passing motorists. Local drivers smile at him broadly which is rather unusual because Fred, when in this mood, often walks down the centre of the road. In the evening he wears expensive clothing and his manner is quite different. He also walks on the pavement like everyone else.

Another character who haunts the Cafe de P pavement is Bill the Basket, a tall, skinny, graveyard-faced chap with an undertaker's expression which gets graver if you haggle too hard for one of the raffia baskets he sells.

Several British residents of Tangier meet at the Cafe de P for a daily chat between 11am and noon. You can't miss them as they usually sit at a window table between the main entrances. Dorothy Leyburn, the former local rep for British Airways, is there most days with her mother, Babs, a one-time actress in Newcastle. They are usually joined by grey-haired Tanger Inn owner, John Sutcliffe, who pops in for coffee and a shoeshine.

Now and then they are joined by others such as the verbally energetic Ian Brown, who was once a VIP chauffeur in Britain ; slow speaking John Gentle, a retired Registrar from Cambridge and Frank Nelson, a slim and dapper chappie with bushy grey moustache and clipped speech as precise as his personal system devised to relieve bookies and casino croupiers of their not so hard earned cash. Mind you, he readily admits that his foolproof system is not proof against fools. Frank has also perfected a fascinating guerrilla warfare conversational technique which he uses, slowly but surely, to wind up those people he thinks should be brought down to earth. His unusual word play utterly confounds conventional thinkers but is a constant source of amusement when you are not on the receiving end.

Others who use the Cafe de P regularly are Tom Govan, a quiet Scot known here as Tom the Pipe because of his distinctive curved pipe ; tall, slim and well-dressed Harry Twentyman, and Maurice Borst from Holland who, along with Britisher Frank Walker, made the Grenouille Restaurant one of the most popular in town.

The Cafe de P is not the only meeting place however. Some prefer to sit in the morning sun outside the Metropole or the Manila, two pavement cafes next to each other just two minutes walk along the Boulevard from the Cafe de P. A few doors away is the smaller Paname which has fewer tables outside but also gets the morning sun. Across the road from the Paname are the Zagora and Esquima coffee places which are popular with locals preferring to sit in the shade on a hot day.

Here, you might find Len Tilley, a retired Australian politician who is, quite naturally, a good conversationalist, chatting with fellow Aussy Tom Lindsay, who once worked for the United Nations in Vienna, and two interesting Americans, the retired lawyer Joe Spector and artist Ralph 'Pat' Paterline.

Further down the Boulevard Pasteur, as you walk towards the post office, there is the Le Claridge which boasts the longest line of chairs and tables along the pavement. Here, at about noon, you might find American artist Robert Barnete brushing up his Spanish, French and

Arabic with Scots-born Bruce Robb, a gentleman journalist of the old school who acts as the local stringer for the London Evening Standard and the Beeb.

A couple of doors past the Le Claridge, on the same side, is La Colombe which serves coffee in cups if you prefer. Upstairs is a favourite meeting place for Tangier's sophisticated teenagers.

If you fancy a quick snort with your lunchtime coffee, pop into the Number One restaurant on the ground floor of the block of flats opposite La Colombe and next to the Hotel Rembrandt. At the Number One bar you might find Tom Seath, an ex-teacher from Canada enjoying friendly banter with Yorkshireman Geoff Bradley and former London couturier Bernard Bragg, or others.

Just past the Rembrandt Hotel is the Atlas pavement cafe often overlooked by tourists but popular with Arabic-speaking British locals such as jovial Les Maud, a retired pharmacist. Here also you might meet Riffi and Captain Zomba, two senior official guides, because the Guides Association headquarters is nearby.

The Atlas is usually crowded inside but there's normally a seat outside under the trees. This place stays open until about 4 am which is great for night owls who fancy a black coffee after a late night drinking session. Some people flare their nostrils at the Cafe Atlas because it is unpretentious, but their coffee is good. And cheaper.

Next to the Atlas is a tiny one-man eating place which serves yummy kebabs or hamburger sandwiches usually until dawn. The Atlas is also a good place to have your shoes shined while savouring a coffee. The shoeshine costs between two and six Dirham, depending on your haggling prowess. But still good value when you know that the three shoeshine girls, yes girls, at Heathrow Airport's Terminal Two charge 95 Pence and still expect a tip on top.

Neanderthal & Other Tourists

When the remains and artifacts of Neanderthal man were unearthed at Tangier's Grottoes of Hercules by the two American professors, Hooker Doolittle and Ralph Nahon in 1936, and the upper jaw of a Neanderthal child was found in the same area by the American anthropologist, Carleton Coon in 1939, scientists hailed the discoveries as the first of their kind in North Africa.

But the Moroccans of today tend to smile about all this. They say you only have to go on the beach during the summer season to discover that the Neanderthals may be long dead but refuse to lie down.

And when they do lie in the hot sand, usually within two hours of flying in, they often stay there until their hairy but delicate white flesh has obtained its full ration of second degree burns. They dive into the sea after eating a huge meal of roasted meat and then wonder why they sink to the bottom suffering agonizing cramp. These Nebbishes also lie low in the sand half drunk as their cubs dash into the sea on lilos at the turn of the tide and end up halfway to Spain.

They expect to find everything exactly as it is at home, but this is not Blackpool or Coney Island. They cannot understand that there is less urgency about day to day matters in this country which almost certainly explains why Moroccans do not suffer heart attacks, ulcers and other stress related ailments. If the bank teller stops attending to you to have a chat with a friend, don't take it as an insult. It's custom, not rudeness.

Not many people are trained anthropologists so a few hints on Neanderthal spotting might come in useful. Many of them walk, eat and think with their mouths open, which makes their tiny foreheads look even smaller. Another giveaway is the strange amount of hair the male species have on their knuckles. There's a good reason for this. As they lope along the Boulevard Pasteur with their beady little eyes searching for bananas and peanuts, you will notice how their knuckles sweep the floor. Neanderthals speak no language. They even grunt their own but fair's fair. They understand figures. Sometimes Dirham but more often curvaceous blondes on the beach who cause them to utter a strange tribalistic high-pitched whistle. Neanderthal women are very jealous. When they hear this two-note mating wolf whistle it provokes all their primeval survival instincts and they bare their gold or black teeth in a fearsome snarl. Though they often weigh two tons, they wear bikinis not quite big enough to blow their noses on and their skinny bleached blonde daughters often wear crimplene mini skirts 12 inches above their knees.

It would be unfair to continue this Neanderthal bashing though because some of the more civilised tourists in Tangier have their moments. We were in the Tanger Inn one night when an American woman who had just flown in from New York turned on her bar stool and asked us "How do you like living here in Algiers ?" Yes, we know it sounds crazy, but this not knowing where they are is a trait peculiar to those Seen-it-Done-it tourists whose whistle stop overnight visits are so fast they hardly have time to breathe never mind think.

Another example was the mauve haired elderly lady heard talking to her husband in the bar at the El Minzah Hotel. She said : "Say, Hank, I didn't know there were so many Arabs in Rome." Hank replied : "No, honey, it was Madrid last night, Tangiers tonight, Rome ain't till tomorrow night".

But the best story about flying to Tangier must be the American businessman based in London who told his secretary to book him a flight to this city.

Arriving at London's Heathrow Airport he was horrified to find himself booked on a flight to North America. When he returned to his office in anger one hour later his secretary sheepishly explained that she had automatically presumed that he was going back to America for his holidays so she had checked the atlas and found Tangier was a small island in Lower Chesapeake Bay. Quite right girl, that place was named Tangier by John J. Smith, an English sea captain who did it in fond memory of our Tangier which he visited in the Seventeenth Century.

Some French tourists also lose their sense of direction. We are indebted to Angus Stewart for this giggle : A distinguished lady with a voice like a duchess once approached a Tangier traffic cop on the Boulevard Pasteur and said : "My good man, you look responsible. When does the next bus leave for Jerusalem ?"

Then there was the Welshman and his wife who entered the Tanger Inn one night. As a conversational ice-breaker, genial host John Sutcliffe asked if they had done anything interesting and the wife answered : "Yes, we went on a lovely day trip to Tetanus".

We love the Yorkshire housewife who, walking past Madame Porte's, pointed to the sign above the door and said to her husband : "It says Salon de The, Jim, but Salon de the what ?" Yes, she gave us all a good laugh, but it's easy to make hilarious errors in French. We once asked for Persil and got parsley, which hardly washes whiter than white.

We turn now to the professional complainers. These are usually the bargain basement hunters who scrutinise all the holiday brochures with a microscope to find the cheapest possible package holiday in Tangier and then, on arriving here, magnify any item not fitting their millionaire dream. They come to Tangier because they were told it's so different, yet after only one day start complaining that it's too different. The food is "not British" and the coffee is French and too strong.

Forgetting they are guests in this country they often complain about Moroccan traditions. They criticise the fact that Moroccan women do not sit drinking coffee at pavement cafes, not realising that women traditionally, and for modesty reasons, keep a much lower profile in this man's man's world. In general, Moroccan women stay at home looking after their families. Some don't even go out to buy groceries. Their menfolk do it for them.

Some tourists complain that most menu cards are in French. They complain about the sea being cold. They even complain about the wind or the rain when they have taken a very cheap winter season holiday here. You name it, they complain about it.

The record for the craziest complainer of all is held by Gary Brandon, the friendly London-born bachelor who is the local rep for Cosmos. Last year he had a strange woman client who fed a large Teddy Bear whenever she ate meals in her five star hotel. Her first complaint was that Teddy didn't like the food. Could he have some honey ? Next day, the woman screamed that some fiend had shaved all the fur off her Teddy Bear. An incredulous Gary Brandon rushed to the woman's room and found poor Teddy lying on the bed. It was true. Someone had used a razor to shave all his hair off. Gary suspected that some member of staff had done it as a practical joke but next day, when the woman complained that someone had broken into her hotel room and slashed all her dresses to pieces, Gary opened her wardrobe and discovered there was nothing wrong with her clothing. Nothing at all. Yet the woman refused to accept she was suffering from delusions and, on her return to Britain, laid another complaint to the headquarters of Cosmos.

Believe it or not, she claimed that while out dancing at a disco, someone had broken into her hotel bedroom and raped her Teddy Bear. Gary Brandon had a cute answer to that. He sent a telex back to Cosmos headquarters in Britain pointing out that the woman had no cause for complaint. If she cared so much for her Teddy Bear, she should have hired a baby sitter to look after him instead of leaving him alone.

From unusually live Teddy Bears we now turn to the bored to death tourists who want entertaining all the time. Some of them can't read, so they want to watch free video films in their hotel all day and play Bingo every night. If there's no Bingo they expect Shirley Bassey to sing with the hotel orchestra. Butlins, with thousands of guests, can afford such stars but Tangier hotels cannot.

The complainers even grumble about the orchestra. When the younger set want loud disco or jazz, the older couples demand a waltz or a fox trot. The orchestra just can't win. If they play a French or Spanish melody you can bet your boots that half a dozen moaners will rush to the manager. What do they complain about ? Incredibly, they claim they can't possibly dance to foreign words like 'Amour, Amour'.

Mind you, Tangier's long-suffering hotel managers may smilingly tell them that there's a couple upstairs who never complain about the lack of entertainment. If they fall for that and ask who, they get a big wink and the one word answer 'Honeymooners'.

English as She is Spoke

According to that respected author Anthony "Clockwork Orange" Burgess, the British have always been suspicious of any man who is a good linguist. Burgess has written that the British associate this ability with "Spies, Waiters and Jewish refugees". But the days are long gone when that smear can be used by the lazy gentry. The British businessman of today knows that if he wants to secure plum contracts in Europe, he has to get out and learn the other chap's language.

In this respect, the Moroccans in Tangier have long been leaders in the field. Every visitor discovers, within minutes of arriving, that young boys in the street can often, in addition to their Arabic, speak English, French, Spanish, Dutch, German and even American. Yes, Tangier has an "American Language Centre" where they teach in English. Tourists often laugh at the mistakes many Tangier street salesmen make in pronunciation and grammar. But let's consider how the locals learnt their English. In most cases with their ears only. From English-speaking tourists. And many of these tourists were Irish, Welsh and Scots. What a way to learn a language. There's many an Englishman who can't understand a word uttered by a broad Scot. And don't forget the tourists who use the dialects of Yorkshire, Devon and London's East End. Familiar to us perhaps, but not to Moroccans. Then we have the Americans who, according to our locals, are the most difficult to understand if they are the kind who do not move their lips when talking.   Many tourists find it impossible to comprehend Arabic script. The Arabic alphabet has 28 characters but each has three different forms depending on its position at the end, middle or beginning of a word. And, of course, Arabic is read from right to left across a page, which explains why the beginning of an Arabic book, to Western eyes, starts on the back page.

You might think Arabic looks like scribble with dots on. Yet don't forget the other side of the coin. The English alphabet is just as puzzling for many Moroccans, but they battle long and hard in an attempt to learn it. Although the people of Tangier are outstanding linguists, they don't always get their written English quite right and one of the entertaining pastimes for British and American tourists is to scrutinise menu cards in local restaurants. Here are some we found :

SOULS BONNE FEMME ... we hoped these were not taken from someone living, as what would life be without a sole.

OUR CHEF'S TART... we hope his wife doesn't find out about her.

SWINE CHOP... an illuminating comment on pork.

STEAMY MUSCLES ... sounded like cheesecake but were in a shell.

RUM BARBER ... Sweeney Todd no doubt.

ARTICHOKE BOTTOMS... getting to the heart of the matter ?

A TON A FISH... must have been one whale of a tuna.

MET A POTATO TOO... what else but meat and potato stew.

BING OF EGOS... had nothing to do with Bing Crosby loving himself as Bob Hoped, but banged up eggs which, hilariously, turned out to be an omelette.

JIM AND TONIC was definitely a man's drink but

KRAFTY CHEESE was not so cunning.

We liked the sign over a cubicle in a Tangier dress shop which said "LADIES CAN HAVE FITS HERE", yet the funniest error must be the local man who had an expensive and glossy brochure printed to publicise all the amenities his hotel offered. The most interesting, for men, was the one promising "A FRENCH WIDOW IN EVERY BEDROOM".

Where Do We Go From Here ?

ALGECIRAS. Spanish seaport founded by the Moors in 713. It is connected to Gibraltar by a thin strip of land and, since the re-opening of the La Linea border gate in February 1985, tourists can pop in and out of Gib daily. The yellow-bottomed "Ibn Batouta" or its sister ferry sail between Algeciras and Tangier twice daily.

ASILAH is an ancient and pretty fishing village 30 miles from Tangier along the scenic Atlantic coast. It once won a prize for being the cleanest town in Morocco and probably still is. The Portuguese harbour is built on Phoenician remains. Best day is Thursday, market day. Walk through the enchanting Kasbah. You do not need a guide and it's impossible to get lost.

Have lunch at one of the many fish restaurants. At the El Espigon you can eat outdoors next to the sea under bamboo awnings in surroundings as sophisticated as any.

This restaurant is right at the end of the promenade walking with your back to the old castle and it is the in-place for rich locals every Sunday lunchtime. Excellent food is provided by Sherif Mohamed

Alaoui el Mrani, who speaks fluent English and goes out of his way to please discerning clients.

If you prefer a quick snack of cheap but super deep-fried sardines and British-style chips, try Pepe's Spanish El Oceano caff which has plastic tablecloths and is opposite the castle. In good weather you can eat in their garden in the shadow of the castle walls. Don't jump if the tame peacocks peck your toes under the table. They are only begging for bread.

CEUTA is your chance to visit Spain without crossing the sea. It's a military station and seaport opposite Gibraltar and a two hour bus drive from Tangier. It's also a Duty Free area and shoppers paradise where liquor is amazingly cheap. Spanish brandy at about £1 a bottle, gin, vodka, bacardi and rum at £2 a bottle and world famous brands of whisky at £3. Many British tourists buy their liquor at the well-stocked and efficient Roma Supermarket, known as Supa Roma, in the main street.

Radios, cameras, calculators and watches are also cheap in Ceuta but watch out for the tricky shopkeepers who put high-priced labels on them to catch unwary tourists from Europe who are used to luxury items being highly taxed. You should definitely haggle when buying the above items in Ceuta. Shake your head vigorously and in most cases the price on the label will be reduced very smartly.

If you are buying on an overseas credit card such as Visa, do not allow the shopkeeper to charge an extra six or seven per cent. Tell him that he's the one who pays that commission to the credit card company. Not you.

Rolex watches are a good buy but watch out for the clever fakes. Another trick used by a few Ceuta shopkeepers is the palming off of faulty cameras, radios and watches. So, when he has demonstrated a good one, don't let him wrap it in case he switches it for a dud.

There's eating places aplenty in Ceuta but for cheap and good stew and chips or fish and chips, try Mustapha's working man's caff next to the luxury La Terraza restaurant in the square called Rafael Gibert.

Some restaurants in Ceuta charge for bread (pan) when you have not eaten any. If so, strike it off the bill and refuse to pay. And watch out for the restaurants offering seemingly cheap main courses but sneakily charging £3 for two portions of chips.

Pesetas are the currency in Ceuta and special coaches go from Tangier regularly for a day trip. See your travel rep for tickets and the bus will call for you at your hotel most likely. Don't forget your passport. Also remember that Ceuta time is different in the summer and if you don't keep your wits about you it's easy to miss the bus back. By the way, if you hire a car in Tangier, don't try taking it to Ceuta. Hired cars cannot normally leave Morocco.

CHAUEN, also spelled Chechaouen and even Xauen, is 120 km from Tangier and high in the mountains. It was founded in the Fifteenth Century by Andalusian regugees who made it into a fortress. Moulay ben Rashid managed to hold it against a massive force of Portuguese which had already taken over Tangier. Its medieval dungeon's last prisoner was the famous Abd el Krim at the end of the Rif War. This tiny "lost village" is pretty, clean and romantic and still rather hidden from modern stresses. It has a classic Spanish plaza which is in sharp but pleasant contrast to its typically Moroccan medina that offers locally made carpets and lovely polished stones gathered from the surrounding crags and canyons. The country people are delightful but don't forget to haggle.

DIP FOREST. A great day can be enjoyed at the Chez Abdou restaurant and holiday garden 17 km from Tangier in the Diplomatic Forest. Slap bang on the fabulous Atlantic Beach with changing rooms, toilets, showers and a kiddies playground, you can eat at tables in the sun or sit cross-legged on cushions in the cool Moroccan room. Superb dishes. Try Tagra, a large whole fish cooked with potatoes, tomatoes, red peppers, garlic and herbs. Choose the fish, probably still gasping, in the courtyard kitchen. Worth renting a car to get to.

MURISSAT. Pronounce it Marie Set and a taxi will take you to a difficult to reach beach just past the new marina at Malabata. Great for tourists wanting to get away from tourists and mingle with extremely friendly Moroccans. Kebabs are cooked right there on the beach and the sea is crystal clear.

MERKALLA BEACH. Nestles in a secluded canyon below the Marshan near the Jew's River. Sidi Mustapha runs the only beach bar and his lunch is simple but good value. The sand on this beach gives relief from Rheumatism, Arthritis and Gout and many Continentals come here just to cover their legs for a few hours each day. Strangely, a vast horde of lobsters crawled out of the sea here in 1930 and refused to leave. Thousands kept coming and for weeks the people of Tangier feasted on this unusual luxury gift from Allah.

THE MIRAGE. Better known as Robinson's, is great if you want a good meal with a really romantic sea view. It's above the famous Grottoes of Hercules on Atlantic Beach 15 km from Tangier and is run by English-born Richard Kemp and his co-director Ahmed Chekkour. If you have lunch at their place they give you access to the private ARABIAN SANDS HOLIDAY CLUB complex next door which is popular with many British tourists. The Arabian Sands has a well-tended swimming pool alongside a pretty bar and overlooking a vast and sandy secluded beach.

Another (seasonal) attraction at the Arabian Sands is their fun CAMEL TREK during which you ride a camel right along that vast beach and then stop for a picnic lunch washed down with free Sangria. There's plenty of time for a swim in the Atlantic but beware of the tricky triple current if you swim far out. Total cost including transport from Tangier and back is about a tenner. See your travel rep for tickets. A camel ride is a great giggle but PLEASE hold tight when he is ordered to stand up because he does so very abruptly.

A couple of miles along the coast, driving towards the Cap Spartel lighthouse, you will find another excellent eatery. This is the SOL BEACH RESTAURANT AND BAR, run by jovial Abdeslem Temsamani who speaks English and quickly makes you feel at home in his efficient and clean establishment. Formerly the private chauffeur to a Paris-based millionaire, Abdeslem specialises in superb fish dishes, particularly his shrimp Paella but we also liked his rabbit in tomato sauce. The SOL is open all year round from 9am to 9pm.

Further along the Atlantic Coast, 43 miles from Tangier and past Asilah, is the delightful little town of LARACHE where Moorish and Spanish architecture blend harmoniously in both the harbour and Kasbah areas. And just across the nearby river Loukos are the ruins of ancient LIXUS, one of the oldest cities in Morocco. It is in this area that legend says the Gardens of the Hesperides, of golden apples fame, were sited.

SUNDAY MARKET. Special coach tours are laid on for day trips to Asilah and most of them call in at the open market on the way back

There is another Sunday Market held by Berbers about 25 miles from Tangier. Great for photographers as the scene is quite Biblical, but tourist coaches cannot go there at the moment because a small bridge leading to the area must be repaired. However, if you wish to visit this market, we recommend you make up a private party of four or more and let Nat Tours take you there. This is a private travel agency run by British-born Dorothy Leyburn and her husband. In fact, if you want any hand-tailored excursion, to places right off the beaten track, contact Dorothy at Tangier 320-68.

TETOUAN is the former capital of the Spanish Protectorates in Northern Morocco. Interesting medina and market place. Good Archeological Museum. A rather Spanish city still with its fountains and balconied houses in the Andalusian style.

TARIFA. On a clear day you can see this bustling Spanish fishing town directly opposite the Tangier beach if you stand with your back to the Rif Hotel. Very Moorish with pretty white houses and narrow winding streets, it's the most southerly town in Spain. You can go by hydrofoil on a 35 minute voyage or by the one hour ferry boat 'Baleares'.

For tourists wishing to go further afield, modern air-conditioned trains and coaches go from here to Marrakech, the second oldest Imperial City ; Rabat, the capital ; Fez, the cultural capital and Casablanca, Morocco's biggest port. Casa, by the way, has the world's biggest sea water swimming pool covering almost nine acres.

When travelling by train, tourists are advised to go first class. Regular flights are also available and tickets can be obtained from the efficient main office of Royal Air Maroc which is opposite the Cafe de Paris.

Day Trip to Gib

Every year, thousands of Britons holidaying in Tangier pop over to the Rock to taste a bit of "Britain in the Sun". If you can afford the little extra, take the highly enjoyable 15 minute air trip - which is the world's shortest intercontinental flight, by the way - and gives you more time for sightseeing, shopping and a typical British pub lunch. Get your duty free fags on the flight back because they are cheaper. We also suggest you take the mini-bus Tour of the Rock laid on by your travel rep because, in the end, it's the cheapest way of touring the whole Rock and it also gets you to the town centre (and back again to the airport) which saves you two taxi trips. You can take the 90-minute hydrofoil voyage which is cheaper but if the wind comes up it does not return - and you are lumbered with the expense of staying in Gib overnight.

What a way to go : But you can sail to Gib on the new Catamaran if you wish. You can, of course, arrange your own voyage but the Rogue advises you to get your day trip tickets to Gib from your package holiday travel reps - because their organised groups swish through immigration formalities far quicker. (That also applies to day trips by road to duty free Ceuta).

Gib is a three mile long and three quarter mile wide chunk of Regency style Britain in the sun which the British captured from the Spanish in 1704 after three days of bitter fighting. It's a highly strategic base and now, the Spanish want it back. Rumour has it that Britain will box clever and return the Rock to the Spaniards if Madrid agrees to let the British lease it on a long term basis, as was done with that other strategic British Colony, Hong Kong.

Nestling in the shade of a 1,400 foot high block of limestone, Gib is a place where you can spend British currency. It has a casino, betting shops, pubs, British cinemas, a Swiss cable car, Hambro's and Barclays Banks, two branches of Liptons and a Main Street full of shops, bazaars, bars and eating places. Most day trippers use taxis but the buses are regular and very cheap.

Money-minded people will be glad to know that financially, Gib is as solid as a rock. For hundreds of years defence was the mainstay of the economy but just lately that has been completely changed. Defence now plays second fiddle to ship-repairing, tourism and the various financial services.

As a result of the full opening of the border with Spain in February 1985, Gibraltar now expects to play host to about three million day trippers every year and that spells great prosperity to the Rock's 30,000 resident population. Quite apart from that, Gib is fast becoming a popular tax haven. Instead of hiding their money in the Cayman Islands or the Channel Islands, the smart expatriates, particularly the British ones living in Spain, are now flocking to bank their savings in Gibraltar. This can be done in a variety of ways, through a trust in the form of a life assurance policy or bond or even by setting up a small tax exempt company.

To avoid United Kingdom corporation or capital gains tax, you can easily set up a company in Gib. It can even be a non-resident company which is tax exempt except for a flat tax fee of £200 a year irrespective of profits.

The six domestic banks, including the Algemene Bank Nederland and the Bank of Credit and Commerce International along with Barclays, the big favourite for Visa card owners, are all entitled to have offshore units. In addition there are the three purely offshore banks, Hambros, the Hong Kong and Shanghai Bank and the Arab-backed Gibraltar and Iberian.

Gibraltar was named after Jebel al Tarik, the famous Moorish conqueror who took it in 711. The first known inhabitant of Gib was a Neanderthal woman aged about 40 who lived in the lower caves. Her grotty skull is in the museum of the Royal College of Surgeons in London. On Gib's backside is the spectacular water catchment of solid concrete covering 37 acres to catch rain and convey it to the town's reservoirs capable of holding 16 million gallons. The large complement of British servicemen and women has its own sea water distillation plant, yet Gib still has to import fresh water, mainly from Morocco but also in regular tankers from the UK which use fresh water as ballast until they reach the Rock and then swop it for sea water.

The surface area of Gib covers only two and a half square miles but inside the Rock there is a vast series of caves and galleries running over 30 miles and it is said these could house a small army of British troops for many months, living on tinned goods, fish and a secret water supply.

There are many interesting places to visit. The Upper Galleries, which were excavated out of the rock as a result of the Great Siege mounted by the French and Spanish from 1779 to 1783, are visually entertaining as well as historical. The Moorish Castle, which still bears the scars of ten sieges, was first built in 711.

One of the most popular sights is St Michael's Cave, 1,000 feet above sea level. This is an enchanting palace of stalagmites, stalactites, an underground lake and a mysterious subterranean breeze which some locals insist blows all the way from Africa through a secret tunnel stretching from Gib to Tetouan in Morocco.

Legend has it that Gibraltar's Barbary Apes know where this tunnel is, but so far they are not talking. The Barbary Apes are not really apes but a breed of monkeys without tails. They have been on the Rock for 800 years and another legend has it that when they leave Gib, so will the British.

And that is why, on 25 August 1941, Winston Churchill sent an urgent message from London expressing his wish that the apes should not be allowed to die out. He sent this signal after the Gestapo mounted a demoralising propaganda story which said that the last few apes were dying.

The apes are a great tourist attraction but please note that they are also cunning pickpockets. They even know how to pinch wrist watches on expanding bracelets, so watch it and keep them at arm's length.

If, like us, you are keen on camping, Gibraltar is disappointing. For some strange reason, whether lack of space, snobbery or just to keep the hotels full, the Rock has no camping park. And even if you have a fully equipped caravan, you are not allowed to sleep in it. The solution is to drive across the La Linea border, sleep there and return to Gib next day.

Another grumble is that car owners who are driving into Gib just to catch the ferry to Tangier cannot buy insurance for one day. The shortest period of car insurance available at the Gibraltar border post is one week. And it's expensive. Why can't they offer a more sensible and far more economic 48-hour car insurance period just like the Spaniards ?

Food for Thought

Package holiday tourists who come to Tangier usually get lunch or dinner thrown in at their hotel and often make do with a small snack in between. In many cases they never eat out at local restaurants which means they are missing a great treat as the standard of cooking is high and all dishes, particularly vegetables, have a fantastic taste. This is mainly due to the fact that Moroccan VEGETABLES are grown naturally and without those horrific chemicals used for fast and forced growing overseas.

Moroccan FARM CHICKENS also titillate the palate because they taste like chickens, unlike often fishy tasting fishmeal fed objects reared overseas under ultra-violet lamps in vast breeding sheds. And the BREAD, whether it is the flat, round wholemeal variety or French, the bread here is no pain. It tastes delicious and is fresh because Tangier bakeries, like the ones in France, produce it three times daily in time for each main meal.

In the streets of Tangier you will often see women or children, rarely men, carrying long flat wooden trays covered with a cloth. Under the cloth is homemade dough on its way to the local baker who charges about 30 centimes for putting it into his oven which is real thrift when you know how cheap bread is in local shops.

Sexy Frenchmen regard CONTINENTAL BREAKFAST as a roll in bed with honey, but in Tangier you normally get only croissants with jam or marmalade. Even if you do have full breakfast you will rarely find British style BACON AND EGGS on the menu because bacon, being pig, is untouchable for most Moroccans. In fact, bacon is not easy to find when you go shopping in this city. It's usually only sold by Spanish butchers and when you do find it the price is rarely less than 50 Dirham a kilo.

If you fancy a good bacon and egg breakfast, try the Windmill beach restaurant where bacon, eggs, tomato, bread and a pot of tea costs just over £1. Emma's BBC beach bar also provides bacon and eggs and so does the Ibis, an unpretentious but popular place in the same street as the Hotel Velasquez just off Bvd Pasteur.

From bacon to ICE CREAM might seem a sudden jump but the two are related. Moroccans rolled their eyeballs in astonishment recently when a published statistic disclosed that 98 per cent of all mass-produced ice cream in Britain   is made from emulsified pig fat. If you wish to taste the pure stuff in Tangier try the parlour next to the seafront Marco Polo Hotel or get a takeaway cornet from the Grenade snack bar next to the seafront Miramar Hotel. The Atlas beach restaurant opposite the Miramar also sells good value takeaway cornets and so does the Coloma Creamery three doors from the Chellah Hotel. All the ice creams mentioned above are vastly superior to the often powdered variety sold in streets from push carts.

Also sold from push carts and street stalls are nuts, cheap sweets and nougat. But the most delicious homemade NOUGAT can be found at the tiny kiosk next to the jewellery shop at 89 Rue Semmarin, just off the Grand Socco.

For those with a different sweet tooth, the PASTRIES in Tangier are superb. The Gazelle's Horn is a crescent shaped pastry filled with ground almonds mixed with butter, cinnamon and dusted with icing sugar. Coconut Macaroons have wild honey inside and experts on HONEY will tell you that the wild Moroccan variety is outstanding. General Franco liked it so much that he had two litres sent by air from Tangier to Madrid every week for the last 20 years of his life. There's a sting in that tale though. Franco kept his love of Moroccan honey rather quiet in order not to risk political problems from the zealous Spanish bee keepers.

As you walk round Tangier you will see street vendors with large shallow and round metal trays containing what, to a Yorkshireman, seems like custard pie. It's actually a mildly salty homemade SAVOURY SNACK made with chickpea flour. Another sight in the Kasbah is something burning in a small clay bowl at the front door of a house. This is a charcoal brazier kept outside until the acrid smoke has disappeared leaving red hot embers perfect for indoor cooking.

In the Grand Socco you will see the WATER SELLER with a goat bladder full of spring water on his back. The water pours through long thin brass tubes attached to the goat's anus and is served in highly polished brass bowls. For a few centimes you get a liberal drink and you might wonder how he can make a living. The answer is that he also gets money from snap happy tourists looking for a uniquely local photograph to take home. That's why he wears often outlandish garb of Berber straw hat with dangling tiny bells, a colourful coat with gay buttons and a heavily studded belt. You get good local colour in your snapshots and he gets your green stuff in his pockets, so both sides are happy. Mind you, the water he sells as being from a mountain spring is usually from the nearest tap.

Not that there's anything wrong with local TAP WATER. It's clean and many Western residents of Tangier can drink it without ill-effect because their tummies are used to the different mineral balance. Most of us Westerners had to learn how to run before we could walk when we first came here. Those who were too old to run, quickly discovered how wise it was to keep a spare wad of loo paper in their pockets in case they got the trots while pottering round town.

If you have a fussy tummy which is easily affected by the different mineral balance in any water away from home, you will keep away from local tap water. Take a tip from Elizabeth Rex who travels round Britain a lot and, to avoid having to run during her highly-publicised walkabouts, always drinks bottled Malvern Water. Her ice cubes are also made from it by the way, even when she has her favourite tipple of Gordon's Gin and tonic.

The Palace advisers make sure the Queen never drinks tap water anywhere and anyone knowing the different mineral balance between the soft water in the South of England and the harder water up North will understand why. When the Queen is abroad in warmer climates she drinks at least two pints of Malvern Water every day and by doing so replaces the body fluids lost by sweating, though the Queen politely calls it "glowing".

If you wish to replace body fluids, try SIDI HARAZEM which is much the same as Malvern Water though the French prefer Vichy and Perrier. If you find the name Sidi Harazem difficult to remember, ask for Sidney Harrison, the laughing shopkeeper will understand. When we first arrived in Tangier, a waiter solemnly told us that this bottled mineral water was lavatory water. It took us some time to work out that he meant laboratory (tested).

Out of every planeload of tourists coming to Tangier in the summer, roughly 25 suffer from funny tummy during their first week. Some rush round screaming food poisoning but that is very rare in this city. Local doctors say that in nearly all cases the stomach has been overworked. Given a good hiding is a better way of describing it, for the following reasons :

ONE. When on holiday we tend to eat more food than we normally do back home.

TWO. Most Westerners are not geared to the different cooking oils and herbs so popular with Moroccan and French chefs. Many hotels in Tangier balance their meals carefully to cater for their mostly British clients but, if you eat outside the hotel, be careful of possibly overspiced dishes or super rich sauces.

THREE Lots of British tourists drink beer during the day and forget that BEER is a laxative when you are not used to it.

FOUR. They drink WINE with their meals. Yet another laxative.

FIVE. FRUIT is very cheap here and hotels usually give you as much as you like. Yet fruit is another laxative.

SIX. To eat lots of fruit and drink both wine and beer on the same day is obviously asking for triple trouble.

SEVEN. While lying sweltering in the hot sun we gulp down several ice cold SOFT DRINKS or natural orange juice. Yet another diabolical assault on our stomachs. Remember that when you are on holiday, your tummy is not. It's working at least six times harder than normal. If you don't take care of your stomach there's a strong chance it will take its revenge by taking a holiday itself.

Should you be unlucky and get gippy tummy with severe abdominal pain it might easily have been caused by taking ANTI-MALARIA TABLETS back home. Experienced travel company reps are convinced there is a definite link, so consult a doctor if you have that problem.

If you get less severe tummy trouble, yet find yourself running a lot, you will usually discover that the tablets you brought with you, and which always solved the problem in the past, fail to seal you up. It often takes the local drug to beat the local bug. Chemists usually prescribe Ercefuryl 200 capsules which cost about 15 Dirham and act within four hours.

The best advice, which only the sensible take, is not to plunge back into normal eating and drinking on the second day when you feel much better. Keep well away from beer, wine, fruit, spicy food and chips. This takes immense willpower when you are convinced you are cured, but remember that it's the drugs in your stomach which are conning your brain into thinking you are better so play it safe, rather than suffering all over again. With double the pain.

Another common curse is SUNBURN. This should be a matter of commonsense, yet some tourists leave their brains at home when they travel abroad. If you have not been abroad before it is important to remember that 20 minutes each side is usually quite enough on your first day during our hot summers. It doesn't seem long but look at your body in the bedroom mirror that night and if you are smart your brain will confirm the accuracy of that.

And Mum, take extra special care with the kids. We tend to forget that sunburn hits noses, cheekbones and shoulders five times quicker when they are playing in the sea or in the shallow end of the hotel swimming pool. Reflect on that. While on the subject of sunbathing, try to cut it out when your tummy is funny. It can hate heat while it's digesting the food you ate.

When your stomach is better, treat it to some COUS COUS. This is a cleverly blended meal of semolina type grains made from hard, durum wheat, each golden grain separated from the other. It is often tinted yellow with saffron and served with stewed meats, vegetables, herbs, and sometimes with nuts, almonds or prunes.

If you see PASTILLA or Bstila on a menu, prepare for a treat. It's a smallish crispy pancake stuffed with chopped pigeon meat, more often chicken, and almonds bonded together with egg and wrapped in layers of thin, flaky pastry. Also contains onion, sugar, coriander, saffron, ginger and cinnamon.

In the summer season many tourists are mystified to see street vendors selling a small green fruit with lumps on. These are known as PRICKLY PEARS and they are the soft fruit of the cactus. But be careful. Do not pick them yourself if you see them growing over a garden wall or out in the country because they are covered in tiny, almost invisible and painful needles. The vendor will peel three or four for you at a cost of about One Dirham and you can eat them right there standing in the street. Deliciously sweet and nutritious.

Another sight puzzling tourists is the street vendor walking round with a long wooden pole covered in a hard creamy substance. It's CARAMEL TOFFEE and he will cut off a small chunk with his flat-bladed knife for one Dirham. Local schoolkids often buy a small chunk for ten centimes.

Exploring the Covered Market behind the Grand Socco you might see another surprising thing. Shopkeepers often have a pretty, delicate ivy-like growth twining up the wall and across the roof. All this growth comes from what appears to be a strange bulb half immersed in small plastic container of water. It's actually a SWEET POTATO and a good idea to copy back home. But change the water every day.

Another thing which is not what it appears to be is the long stalked vegetable that looks like celery. In fact, it's the outer stems of the ARTICHOKE and they are used to delicious effect in local meat stews.

No visit to Morocco would be complete without trying HARIRA which is an elaborate soup of chopped mutton, onion, chickpeas, tomato, chicken livers, eggs, ginger and coriander. It's very filling and there is a good reason for its popularity. Locals eat it to pack their stomachs and carry them through the daylight hours during the Holy month of Ramadan, in which Moroccans allow nothing to pass their lips from dawn to sunset. Not even water or mint tea.

Tourists either love or hate MINT TEA. The way to hold a hot glass of mint tea is with the thumb on the rim and the forefinger on the bottom. Of the glass, that is. In a Moroccan home the preparation and drinking of mint tea is a lengthy ritual and it is wise to make loud, even rude, sipping noises when your host asks you to taste the first glass from the pot. This loud slurping and lip-smacking shows your pleasure and pleases him also. Him, because Dad usually makes the tea for guests, not Mum.

If you like mint tea, buy some GREEN TEA at any bacal for about five Dirham. Back home, place two teaspoons in a teapot with mint on top. Pour boiling water over the mint raising and lowering the kettle as you do so because this oxygenates the water and vastly improves the taste. Stir, add sugar then leave to brew for a couple of minutes. Serve in glasses, not cups. Some people scent mint tea with orange blossoms but if you are rich, buy some ambergris instead. This is one upmanship of a very high order indeed.

AMBERGRIS is a wax-like substance found floating in tropical seas and chunks as big as a football, worth several thousand dollars, are often found in the intestines of the sperm whale. It is valuable because it's used as the main base for quality perfumes but few Westerners know it can be used in mint tea. In rich Moroccan homes they keep a small piece of ambergris, worth about £20, in a small tin and surrounded by cotton wool. The minutest bit of cotton wool is taken from the tin and placed in the mint tea to impart a delicate smell to the brew.

If you want to buy some ambergris, go and see English-speaking Soulaimane Madini who runs that excellent perfume shop at 14 Rue Sebou.

Bull's Feet & Frog's Legs

Some tourists shudder when they see big hairy amputated bull's and COW'S FEET on sale while walking round the Grand Socco. Their first thought is usually "How could anyone eat such awful looking things?"

Yes, they do look rather grotty but make a dish fit for a prince when cooked. After being de-haired, two feet are placed in a pot with chickpeas, beans, potatoes, onion, sweet red peppers, four eggs and various spices as well as garlic. The pot is then taken to the oven at the local bakery and allowed to cook gently overnight for about eight hours.

When served the meat, which peels off the bone easily, is very juicy and Moroccans will smilingly tell you that bull's feet stew is good for a man on his honeymoon. Another energy giving local delicacy is

73

CAMEL'S HEAD, whether baked or roast. The brains and tongue are said to be such good aphrodisiacs that, in the immortal words of one Cordon Bleu chap we know : "You make two sons that night for sure and then sleep like a baby".

Today, many people are familiar with French delicacies although it's not that long ago when untravelled Westerners grimaced at the French practice of eating SNAILS. Now, however, they are served in many top British and American restaurants and posher grocery stores stock tins of them with the shells sold separately.

Another unusual delicacy adored by the French is a dish of SEA URCHINS, those porcupines of the ocean feared by barefoot bathers. The coral tinted flesh is scooped out with a teaspoon and eaten raw, flavoured only with a few drops of lemon juice.

Another creature raised to a lordly place on the Frenchman's table is the common or garden frog. Most Britishers freak out at the thought of eating FROG'S LEGS but the normally conservative American is becoming so interested in them that they can now be bought in deep frozen packs at supermarkets.

If you have never eaten frog's legs, why not be adventurous and try some ? The best place in Tangier is named the Grenouille which, for those who don't know, is French for frog. This is a superb little restaurant opposite the Rembrandt Hotel where you can have 24 frog's legs at a most reasonable price. If you can forget that frogs croak, eat flies and have slimy green and spotty skins, you might find their legs tasting rather like baby chicken. They are about two inches long and are usually skinned and prepared in such a way that the two legs stay fastened together so that you can pick up the two tiny ankle bones with both hands and, in one bite, tear off the deliciously tender little thighs.

If, in spite of all that propaganda on behalf of frog's legs, you still don't consider them right for your palate, bear in mind the fact that they are one of the popular items sold at Harrods, that Egyptian-owned posh people's store in London's Knightsbridge where, for the last 15 years, tinned locusts, African worms, snake meat, kangaroo tails, birds nest soup (mostly spit and mud) and even caterpillars from Hong Kong have been sold. So what's so unusual about bull's feet ?

Good Eating Places

Tangier has a profusion of good restaurants and cafes to choose from but if you appreciate advice then this chapter might help. The Rogue's Guide Guide has tested and can recommend several. Having said that, we must hastily add the insurance clause that any eating place not mentioned should not feel in any way slighted. We selected the ones below to give readers a personal selection which includes the most expensive, the cheapest, the most popular and the unusual.

If you are looking for a restaurant where most of the staff speak English, try RUBIS GRILL opposite Madame Porte's tea salon. If you are a teetotaller, don't be shy, there's nothing to stop you having a cup of coffee or a lemonade at the bar. Some British residents pop in for a snort at lunchtime.

At most bars in Tangier, particularly on the beach, they serve tappas. That's the Spanish word for small plates of assorted tit bits like deep fried sardines, squid, baby sole, tomato and potato salad etc. TAPPAS are supposed to be free but in some bars they load the price of beer with an extra Dirham to stop you getting owt for nowt. As a general rule, if you order an alcoholic drink at a beach bar, ask them pointedly whether they serve tappas. And in many places you have to keep asking for them as they are slow to arrive. In the hope, perhaps, that you might forget.

For good local cooking in a homely atmosphere at reasonable prices, try the MIRAMAR HOTEL on the beachfront next to the Rif Hotel. It has a modern and clean kitchen where the owner, Mohamed Drisse, will arrange a special Spanish Paella if you give him advance notice. The barman, Ahmed Elaouffi, is married to an English girl and he speaks English and four other languages fluently. The Miramar has a glass sun porch outside which is popular for morning coffee, afternoon tea or a quick snack of egg and chips.

For Chinese, Vietnamese and vegetarian dishes, the LA PAGODE at 3 Rue el Boussiri, just up the road across from the Cafe de Paris, is a must. We often pop in for a light lunch starting with delicate tea, then Spring Rolls full of beef with rice gently laced with soya sauce and a small bowl of unusual but tasty salad. We finish with more tea and the price per person is about 20 Dirham. Closed Monday.

For Indian food and also vegetarian dishes, try the luxury EL KHAYYAM on the seventh floor of the seafront Almohades Hotel. Expensive, but their Mutton Curry Baghdad or Tandoori Chicken are good value.

For Spanish dishes and tasty fish, try ROMERO'S in Avenue Prince My Abdellah, the street off the Bvd Pasteur just opposite Le Claridge.

If you wish to take a discerning Moroccan out for a meal we recommend two places. THE EUCALYPTUS Restaurant is 6 km from Tangier in the fashionable forest of R'Milat on the road to the Cap Spartel Lighthouse. Aziz, the patron, gives good food and service and also provides a free and popular kiddies playground. Closed on Mondays in the winter season. The other popular Moroccan rendezvous which Westerners also like is RAIHANI'S at 10 Rue Ahmed Chaouki, the little street opposite the Paname in the Bvd Pasteur. Raihani's offer good kebabs, tagine and cous cous, but they also have a three course French menu for tourists. Clean tablecloths. Open every day.

Across the road from Raihani's there is the SAN REMO at number 15 where they specialise in superb Italian dishes. Run by Chez Toni, this is an extremely popular place for local gourmets and socialites. Give 12 hours notice and you get Toni's speciality, DRESSED CRAB. Clothed Monday.

Another place for Italian pizza is the MARSA, a brand new red-tiled Spanish hacienda on the sea front next to the B.P. garage and opposite the railway track. The Marsa has a great sun balcony overlooking the sea and the railway station. By the way, if you want to take a shortcut to the city centre, go up the steps in Rue Ibn Zohr, the tiny alley next to the Marsa Pizza house.

Also on the sea front in the Avenue d'Espagne is the pretty little German run MARCO POLO HOTEL which is diagonally opposite the private Yacht Club on the beach. The Marco Polo gives good value and service. Try their English-style toasted ham and cheese sandwiches sitting on a charming open sun balcony. Speciality of the house is a Filet Marco Polo stuffed with ham and cheese. Right next to the Marco Polo is a tiny alley which is another good shortcut to the city centre which brings you to the Hotel Rembrandt very quickly.

For excellent French cuisine, the GRENOUILLE, already mentioned as the place for frog's legs, is very popular with British and American locals. The three course menu, which has the widest choice in town, is terrific value and they sell wine by the carafe. Closed Monday. Their main competitor is the GAGARINE just behind the post office. It has a Swiss chalet style decor with intimate candlelit tables also offering a good three course tourist menu.

Slightly more expensive but most popular with the real gourmets is the NAUTILUS, five doors up from the Velasquez Hotel. Try the unique Peanut Soup or the super Paté. Then Pepper Steak or tender chicken kebabs. Another quality dish is Duck in Orange Sauce, a recipe personally given to the Nautilus by the famous international chef, Robert "Baby Face" Carrier. Closed Tuesdays but every other day its excellent service and ambiance is due to the owner, Rachid Temsamani, a former antique dealer who opens the popular Nautilus beach restaurant during summer months.

For an international cuisine try the NEGRESCO at 20 Rue Mexique, just across the road from the Cafe de Paris. The Paella Valenciana is a special dish for two at a reasonable price. Fried Octopus and Squid is great here and they also have a fast snack bar next door where they give free tappas when you order a beer.

Another popular place is the DOLCE VITA also known as CHEZ LARBI at 18 Rue Mohammed Abdou, near the Mauritania Cinema. Economical tourist menu. We like their rabbit.

For those liking French home cooking without too many fancy sauces there's no better place than GUITTA'S which is opposite the beautiful mosque in Place Kuwait, a two minute taxi ride from the Cafe de Paris. Mercedes Guitta of Swiss extraction has turned her private house into a restaurant for discriminating clients and she also serves meals at tables in her private garden if the weather is good. Her English-style pub bar is popular, particularly with Americans.

For a lighter and cheaper meal, try LES COPAINS, the small log cabin in Rue el Antaki which leads up from the seafront starting from the Marco Polo Hotel. The LES COPAINS specialises in pancakes of all types, all excellent value and starting from 5 Dirham. Opposite the pancake place is THE PINERO which has the slogan "English Tea As Mother Makes it" painted on the front window. Good for fish and chips and you can eat at tables along the pavement.

The MECHOUI ORIENTAL sounds a bit Far East but it's run by friendly Amsterdam-born Willie and her husband, Lahcen, and they serve tasty egg and chips, fish and chips and even takeaway chips in the arcade alongside the Algemene Bank at 48 Blvd Pasteur. Right next door is ERIC'S HAMBURGER joint which is open 24 hours and good for an after midnight snack when most other places are closed.

If you fancy a quick snack but can't be bothered to sit in a cafe, most bacals will make a quick and cheap takeaway sandwich by slicing open a French loaf and filling it with tinned tuna, sardines, or cheese, but the cheapest snacks of all are the hard boiled eggs sold by some bacals at one Dirham each. Peel the shell off and dip the egg into the free bowl of salt mixed with Cummin. If your local bacal doesn't provide this luxury, go to the tiny fruit shop dead opposite the main post office. This shop is number 54, which you will see from the engraved number in the doorstep.

For takeaway dessert, all bacals sell the local yoghurt. The strawberry or pineapple in fluted packs are superb. For takeaway sandwiches you can also try the SANDWICH BAR at 14 Rue Mexique, opposite the Lufthansa office or the GRENADE snack bar near the beachfront Miramar Hotel or the FOUR SEASONS across from the Tanger Hotel in town. All three sell chip butties.

Some tourists think twice about going into the Petit Socco or the Grand Socco for a simple but very cheap meal of kebabs on skewers, or liver with scrambled eggs in one of those tiny holes in the wall, but give it a try. The meat is very clean.

For instance, look in front of the taxi ranks in the Grand Socco. On your left is the Mendoubia Garden which houses the Palace of Justice and, just inside the gateway, Tangier's biggest and most unusual tree.

To the right of the Mendoubia is the BMCE bank at number 55. Right next door you will see an ordinary worker's pavement caff with six blue topped plastic tables outside where only coffee, mint tea and soft drinks are served. Order a Coffee Zizwa which is hot, black and super sweet.

If you are there from 5pm onwards they don't mind if you order tasty lamb kebabs and fresh bread from the CAFE GHOLETTI right next door for less than £1. What's the bet you feel like ordering more kebabs ? And, while sitting there, watch the astonishing scramble for taxis at the green taxi rank. Great free entertainment for Westerners who know what the word queue means. Try forming a queue here and you will quickly realise it's the survival of the fittest. We are not so fit so we solve the problem by paying one of the many fast youngsters a Dirham and he grabs a taxi for us.

Back to food - another place for yummy Moroccan snacks is THE OLD SULTAN'S PALACE with panoramic windows high in the Kasbah and an interesting museum below.

While researching this book, hundreds of British (and American, before the Libyan bombing,) tourists told us that their best Moroccan meals had been savoured at HAMADI'S and the DAR TAGINE. Both serve a five-course fixed menu of typical local food such as Harira Soup and Cous-cous etc, for about a Fiver and both have resident musicians who love posing with you for photographs, so take your camera.

At night, the best way to HAMADI'S, which is at the end of Rue Italy and the beginning of Rue Kasbah, below the Grand Socco (Big Market) is to take a taxi. Good food and good service.

To reach the DAR TAGINE you have to be more adventurous. Ask a taxi to take you there and depending on how crowded the streets are he will drop you as near as possible to the Petit Socco (Small Market). In the Petit Socco square you will find the Cafe Centrale. Next to it is a small tabac (a shop selling cigs and tobacco). Next door is an archway. Walk through slightly to the right and you should see the narrow Rue du Commerce in front of you. Lost already ? OK, ask any small kid to take you, for one or two Diddums (C.O.D.) to the DAR TAGINE at number 29.

Also great giggles are the MOROCCAN EVENINGS mounted weekly by such hotels as the RIF, CHELLAH, PASADENA, and SOLAZUR. (The latter also holds weekly Barbeque Evenings or Gala Dinners.) For about eight quid you get a good cabaret and a typical four-course Moroccan meal. Wine is often thrown in free but go slow on the vino with the Harira Soup as the two can clash.

Many tourists dress up in their newly purchased Moroccan garments, particularly women keen to test those Caftans, but shy husbands can make do with a Fez on their heads. This dressing up adds to the fun at Moroccan Evenings and also provides super giggle photographs to be shown to the neighbours back home. If you don't own a camera you can buy photographs from the freelance cameramen who attend most of the Moroccan Evenings at the big hotels. And, here's a really valuable tip :

When you see the photographs taken by the freelancers you might like one so much that you decide to ask him to print up another copy. Our advice is DON'T, because the copy might not be ready before you leave Tangier (or even this Earth).

Instead, offer to buy the negative and the odds are that he will part with it for about 10 Dirham. Then, when you return home, you can get copies made quicker and cheaper. If the photograph in question shows hubby fondling a busty belly dancer, which it (and he) often does, why not have dozens of copies made and send them out as Christmas cards. Alternatively, keep the negative in the safety vault of a bank as possible divorce evidence. Divorce Court lawyers (and the tit and trivia Sunday newspapers) love that kind of ammunition.

Rather more discreet are the Moroccan Evenings staged at Tangier's elegant EL MINZAH HOTEL with belly dancers performing on Tuesdays and Fridays. Closed Monday. If you give 12 hours notice, the El Minzah provides pigeon in all its glory. Don't wrinkle your nose. Pigeon with Pears is fantastic. Pigeon with Almonds and Onions or Pigeon with Vermicelli is equally tasty. If you wish to taste El Minzah luxury without spending too much money, have tea or coffee by their super swimming pool and watch the wealthy wallowing in it.

TEA SALONS are plentiful in Tangier but the best known is MADAME PORTE. The Madame who started it is long dead but her legend lives on through the excellence of her mouth-watering cakes and pastries. Here, you can also buy those famous British brown loaves bearing the genuine HOVIS imprint.

Another good place for cakes is LA COLOMBE which has smoky glass windows and is opposite the Rembrandt Hotel. Their ice cream is particularly good, unlike some other places where they keep the ice cream in the same fridge as fish and the pong of sardines permeates and spoils the creamy taste.

The SEMIRAMIS Cafe, which is underneath the Royal Automobile Club and next door to the Cafe de France (opposite the Cafe de Paris) has 20 varieties of delicious pastries and is worth looking into if you are not a weight watcher.

ON THE BEACH. It is not possible to say which is the most popular bar or restaurant on the Tangier beach because tourists decide this for themselves. The situation fluctuates weekly with every new wave of summer holidaymakers. A bar which was packed out one week might find itself not so popular the next. In any case, each place has its own character and you should choose the one suiting you and your pocket.

Keeping money in mind it is worth knowing that Mohamed Mojahid, the patron of THE WINDMILL beach place opposite the Solazur Hotel, tells us that if you are accompanied by an official guide, repeat official, the guide gets his lunch on the house at no extra cost to you. A wise idea which we suspect will quickly be copied by other places.

Some hotels run their own beach places, such as the delightful complex recently opened by the CHELLAH, but Rif Hotel clients seem to favour Emma's BBC BAR just opposite their hotel.

At the time of writing the only beach place to remain open all year round is the SUN BEACH opposite the Miramar Hotel. A good tip. Do not walk on the beach further than the last beach establishment as you might be accosted by oddballs, which includes tourist oddballs. And don't walk on the beach after dark if you are straight, mate.

During the day you should experience no hassles on the main beach because there is a tall, glassed in tower opposite the Almohades Hotel. This is a police post usually manned by officers using binoculars and they keep in constant touch with their colleagues on the beach beat. Underneath the observation tower there is a first aid centre during the summer season.

One of the great pleasures at beach bars is that you can wear just about anything. However eccentric. Nobody minds. The same applies to restaurants in town. Hardly anyone dresses for dinner these days. Even in the best restaurants a man can wear an open necked shirt although the ladies mostly like to dress up, often in their newly purchased caftans. If you brought your tuxedo and black tie, Bert, forget it. Unless you are going to a fancy dress party.

FOOTNOTE. *All the information about eating establishments in this chapter held true at the time of going to the printer, but the Rogue's Guide does not hold itself responsible for bad days, problems or changes made since. This includes ownership changes, bankruptcy, a Third World War, new waiters or just inflation. And while on that subject, the Dirham was nearly 12 to the Pound and 10 to the Dollar when this guide was written.*

Cheers Dears

Many tourists bring one or two bottles of duty free liquor to Tangier, which is a good thing because hard tack is expensive in local shops due to high import duty.

Local wine and beer however is not dear and a good place to buy is 63 Rue Holland which is first left up the Rue Belgique walking with your back to the Cafe de Paris. The genial owner is Spaniard MIMON BENDAHAN who makes sure that all bottles in his store are price labelled so there's no haggle problem. Moroccan brewed beer, by the way, swills down much better when you know it is far cheaper than imported brands.

Mimon sells good red and rose plonk at about £1 in no-deposit, throwaway plastic bottles or, if you have a finer palate, consider the better quality wines costing from 13 to 40 Dirham. Mimon is open every day from 10am to noon and he speaks reasonable English.

Two other places selling wine and beer at fair prices are CASA PEPE, a posh little delicatessen next door to Rubis Grill and opposite Madame Porte, or the tiny grocery shop at number 54, Boulevard Mohammed V. This is the shop opposite the post office which sells hard boiled eggs dipped in salt and cummin.

If you order French wine or French champagne in Tangier hotels and restaurants, remember they are subject to high import duty. In one classy restaurant we know they charge 800 Dirham for a bottle of Dom Perignon champers. For an inexpensive bubbly, try MOROCCAN CHAMPAGNE which is fun if you are not pretentious and looks very impressive in an ice bucket on your table.

Liquor served in Tangier's bars and hotels may seem expensive in comparison with the cheap cost of living but please keep in mind that prices are invariably laid down by Government depending on a hotel's star rating. This is not at all surprising. In fact it's quite wise in a country where the larger percentage of the population do not drink alcohol. Another thing worth remembering is that nearly all measures served in local bars are either club size, that's one and a half British tots, or doubles. Very reassuring to remember when you go out for a booze up.

Although most Arabic people do not drink liquor it is fascinating that the English word booze comes from the Egyptian word BOOZAH, the name of a type of beer brewed there for some 3,000 years. Worth mentioning when you go to your local boozer back home for the weekend booze up perhaps.

Equally interesting is that the word alcohol derives from the Arabic term al-Kohl which, for some long lost reason, comes from the word Kohl, the name of a fine powder used to paint the eyes to reduce the sun's glare. This perhaps explains where the phrase 'getting blind drunk' originated.

Most Americans know a Julep is a cold drink of spirits, sugar, bruised mint and ice, but how many know the name comes from Julab, th Arabic word for rosewater. Every American backwoodsman worth his salt knows what a Still is for but many still don't know where Still came from. The secret is that it derives from the word Alembic, which was a medieval Still made from metal or glass and Alembic comes from the Arabic 'al-inbiq' which, of course, means The Still.

When the French took over Morocco in 1912 they immediately planted vineyards. The principal ones are around Rabat and between Meknes and Fez. While a large volume of concentrated grape juice is exported to Britain for conversion to wine, there's plenty of grape left over for us. The rough red plonk here is far better than that cheap foreign red often sold in Britain which sneakily contains chemicals slipped in to make it redder, as the crystal sediment often shows. And Moroccans would not dream of adding anti-freeze chemicals to wine as is done by some unscrupulous wine growing countries.

The more popular red wines are Cabernet, Ksar, Vieux Papes and Sidi Larbi but if you want to take a classy red on a picnic, get a bottle of Cabernet Medallion 1978 from the shops for about £3.

Of the white wines the popular ones are Valpierre, Chaudsoleil, and L'Oustalet though gourmets might fancy the Semillant Blanc de Blanc. Most gourmets sneer at Rosé but there's a treat in store for them here if they buy a deeply chilled bottle of GRAY ROSE which is unique. The grape used for this wine only grows near Casablanca and Meknes, the latter area producing the slightly better quality.

When it comes to hard tack, a favourite drink in Tangier is a Tanger Up, which is a tot of brandy in a large glass topped up with ice and Coca Cola. But when you ask for a brandy and Coke anywhere in this city perhaps you might make a point of specifying SPANISH BRANDY because French costs twice as much.

Sexy tourists can try a Between The Sheets, a cocktail of brandy, rum, orange liqueur and lemon juice and a Bumbo is a very gay drink of rum with sugar.

On that sweet note we reach Closing Time which is not a drink but the saddest moment for all dedicated drinkers. Yet not to forget there's always another way out. They can follow the example of the Duke of Clarence who, in the Fifteenth Century, dived into a 126-gallon vat of Malmsey wine and drowned. What a way to go.

Characters of Yesteryear

In its heyday, Tangier really was an incredible Sinville on Sea, full of villains, smugglers, exiled writers, tax-avoiding American millionaires, on the run SS officers, Vichy French, drug addicts, disgraced bluebloods given a monthly allowance for keeping out of England, paedophiles with long police files and a wide variety of spies and counter spies. Some of the old characters are still talked about in pavement cafes and bars.

PAUL AXEL LUND was the son of a respectable Birmingham family who had a good start in life but went wrong and ended up serving eight years in jail, two of them on Dartmoor.

In January 1954 he came to Tangier as a wanted man on the run from police in the North of England and opened a small, six-stooled drinking spot in the centre of town named the Bar Navarra which became quite notorious as a meeting place for shady characters and oddballs, your author included, as well as tourists.

Paul's stories, told as he drank neat brandy and spat theatrically into a spittoon, kept him busy and surrounded by a wide variety of gullibles from all walks of life. As the bar prospered, Paul's stories grew taller. The tallest being that he had been involved in the mystery double explosion in the Tangier harbour in 1957 when the British-owned motor vessel the "Barra" and a similar vessel "The Red Witch" were blown out of the water.

Both had been fitted with special engines to give them extra speed and Paul claimed they were owned by Britishers smuggling American cigarettes from Italy to Spain via Tangier. Paul said the boats had been blown up by locally based and rival smugglers but political sources tell a different story. This is that both boats had allegedly been used to smuggle arms and ammunition to rebels fighting the French in Algeria and after a Tangier-based French Intelligence operative named "FRENCH CHARLES" had tipped off Paris, two French cruisers had anchored outside the port so that frogmen could swim underwater and secretly attach limpet mines to both the Barra and the Red Witch. Six hours later, when the French cruisers had long sailed away, both boats were blown to pieces, killing a nightwatchman and making world headlines with cleverly planted stories that misled most people to believe it was just a "smugglers' vendetta".

Paul Lund's greatest admirers were the idle rich remittance matrons who lived in Tangier and sat enthralled as he recounted his tall tales judiciously laced with underworld jargon and Cockney rhyming slang. Only one lady customer had any impact on Paul., This was Carol, an attractive and intelligent girl from the most respectable of families. She realised Paul was not the hard nut he claimed to be. In turn, Paul was captivated by this cultured and elegant girl from good stock. They were married and Carol was clearly a good influence because Paul toned down his language and cut down on his drinking.

One of Paul Lund's friends was ERROL FLYNN, the handsome American film star who won World War Two single-handed in so many Hollywood movies. Ironically, in real life Errol Flynn was a spy for the Nazis and anyone who doubts this should read the astonishing book "Errol Flynn, the Untold Story" by the brilliant American author Charles Higham and published by Doubleday in 1980.

Flynn came to Tangier on his luxury 118-foot yacht Zaca and loved to sit in Paul Lund's bar swopping stories as he drank neat Bourbon straight from a bottle.

In 1966 Paul Lund died choking in blood when one of his lungs collapsed. Typically, most people were sad that another odd character had passed on. The fact that Paul was an oddball didn't really matter because in this city, eccentrics were quite the norm. In that respect, Tangier is much the same today. The only thing odd here is to be normal, because that's boring. All the intelligent Westerners living in Tangier today are quite definitely eccentric in one way or another, in the dictionary sense of being either odd, irregular or just whimsical. And the most marvellous aspect of this is that our eccentricity is not only tolerated by Morocccans, but instinctively understood by them.

One famous eccentric who lived in Tangier was RUPERT CROFT-COOKE, who ably documented Paul Lund's life story in a book entitled "Smiling Damned Villain" which is a must for those wishing to understand the criminal mentality. During WW2, Rupert was in the Intelligence Corps, for which he was awarded the British Empire Medal. After the war he was caught in bed with a young male friend and London Society dropped him like a hot brick when he was jailed in Wormwood Scrubs.

On being freed, Rupert retaliated by writing a book about his homosexuality and the criminal conviction this had brought him. Sarcastically entitled "The Verdict of You All" the book was quite sensational for the early Fifties as it pointed out that the antiquated laws on the subject of homosexuality were hypocritical. This made Rupert a total outcast from straight society so he settled in Tangier with Joseph Susei Mari, a highly intelligent young Hindu who acted as his secretary and companion but was a talented author in his own right.

In 1956 Rupert's next book was published. Entitled "Tangerine House" it was full of praise for Tangier. During the next decade Rupert wrote several books including "Seven Thunders" which was filmed. Another book "Bosie" was a brilliant whitewashing job on Lord Alfred Douglas, the former lover of the jailed Oscar Wilde. Rupert was well suited to write this book as he had been friendly with Douglas for 25 years.

In 1970, when his love for Tangier turned sour, Rupert wrote "The Exiles" which, although it claimed to be fiction, was the most vitriolic attack ever made on local British and American residents. His pen portraits were mostly accurate but incredibly bitchy and although he used false names, every character was instantly recognisable and Rupert became the most hated writer in this city.

In 1974 he delivered another devastating attack on local Britishers when he wrote "The Caves of Hercules" which was rightly denounced by the Journal de Tanger as "an evil and cowardly book   because Rupert had quit Tangier. After various trips he settled in the South of England where he died a few months later.

Rupert Croft-Cooke had one main weakness. He was an intellectual snob who sneered at the "ignorant masses and tradespeople". This flaw was used to devastating effect by a Tangier-based journalist when Rupert died. The journalist discovered and exposed the strange fact that Rupert, using a pen name, had secretly written many trashy cowboy and thriller paperbacks for schoolboys over a period of 15 years as a way of making the extra money he needed to keep up his image as a gentlemanly man of letters. The journalist who exposed this fascinating tit bit was GEORGE GREAVES, yet another Tangier character.

An Australian, George settled in this city in the Thirties and, as the local stringer for the British Daily Express and its sister Sunday, reigned supreme as the journalist who knew Tangier better than anyone. A tall, Falstaffian figure with barrel belly and a long white beard, George was equipped with an intuitive knowledge of human nature which gave him an X-ray view of everyone. His tongue was ferocious and instantly deflated inflated egos. He was known as the Great Debunker who was so cynical that he would often say "Every damned thing in this crazy world is shoddy, crooked or fake". A critic once described George as a bitter and twisted man who would die without a friend in the world. This was proved wrong when, at the age of 84, George lay sick in his Rue Goya bachelor flat. He was broke, with his rent overdue for several months and a large telephone bill unpaid. When this became known, members of the local British community rallied to his support and started a collection. Donations poured in and paid most of George's bills and then another collection was started to raise money so that he could return to his native Australia. But in May 1983, George died while being cared for by a loyal young Moroccan friend who had been his companion for many years.

George Greaves may have been a world-weary cynic who was hated and feared by many in his heyday, but one fact should be added to give a fairer picture. Throughout WW2, when Tangier was a neutral city under Spanish control, it was a hotbed of espionage where George worked full time for British Intelligence. As a journalist spy he collected much valuable information for the Allies.

In early 1942, Whitehall became aware that the Germans had a secret signalling post in a house overlookng the vitally strategic Straits of Gibraltar. Using infra-red equipment a group of German Secret Service operatives flashed regular instructions to a German submarine hidden round the coast near the Caves of Hercules which resulted in losses to Allied shipping. An intelligence colleague of George Greaves planted a bomb in that signalling post late one night and blew it up, killing the SS men inside.

In retaliation, the German Secret Service in Tangier organised a revenge bombing. They planted their bomb on the dock alongside Mr S. Silva, a messenger of the British Legation, who was collecting diplomatic bags from the incoming Gibraltar ferry on 5 February 1942. In the blast, Mr Silva and 33 others were killed. The German bomb was made by an Italian and the timing device was constructed by a Swedish clockmaker living in Tangier. Both were congratulated by the German SS for fixing such a great bomb, but the truth was that their bomb was actually a tiny one which wouldn't have caused so much havoc. The reason so many died was that the German bomb ignited plastic explosives which were being smuggled into Tangier in the British diplomatic bags for the use of local British Intelligence men. George Greaves used to pose the question : ''If any victim's relative could have sued for compensation, which government should they have sued ?''.

Another man who spied in Tangier was a friend of George Greaves whose name was Joseph Kimfull. Mention the name Kimfull and hardly anyone will know who you are talking about. But say he was known as DEAN and then watch the reaction from Tangier veterans. A slim and dapper man, Dean had high cheekbones and slightly slanted eyes which, along with his ebony skin, made his face not only pleasing but interesting. If you had spoken to him by telephone without having met him, you would have pictured someone totally different as he sounded posher than Jeeves, the valet of P.G. Wodehouse fame.

Very few people know the truth about Dean's background because he rarely talked about his past and even when he did, his story differed which was his way of telling nosey parkers to mind their own business. Perhaps that is why his friends glamourise him as the son of an elegant Frenchwoman who had a romantic affair with a rich Egyptian while her Lancashire cotton merchant husband wasn't looking, and Dean's critics smear him as being the result of a one-night stand between a woman who kept a British boarding house and a passing through West Indian merchant seaman.

While nobody in Tangier seems able to come up with any proof about either story, there is no doubt that Dean enjoyed a very good education in Britain and that he was quite well connected in his youth, which shows there was money somewhere. Yet in contradiction, it is known that Dean worked as a barman in Germany, France and Monte Carlo before coming to Tangier in the Thirties to be a barman at the El Minzah Hotel. In 1946 he branched out on his own and opened Dean's Bar just down the road from the Minzah and strategically opposite the old British Post Office. From then on he was known to all as Dean of Dean's Bar.

It was a small place, some called it rather tatty, but it quickly became known to the International Set and everybody who was anybody, and nobodies wanting to be seen as somebody, simply had to make a point of popping in for drinks at cocktail time or when collecting their mail at lunchtime. Sadly, Dean died in 1963 after sniffing too much of the white stuff but he was buried with great dignity and much fondness in the British churchyard. In a modest little grave bearing the name "Dean" right next to the ex-crook, Paul Lund, which would have offended Dean's highly sensitive nature.

Shortly after he died, rumours started circulating that Dean had been a spy for the British but few of his admirers believed it. "Spying is a dirty game and Dean was too much of a gentleman to indulge in anything like that," they said. But it was true and Cyril Connolly, the well-informed London literary lion, confirmed it in 1970 when he wrote a preface for Robin Maugham's book "The Wrong People" and stated :" Dean had beautiful manners and an Oxford accent of the old school.. more impressive... he had worked for our Intelligence throughout the war".

Another former British agent who lived in Tangier for several years and happened, perhaps not coincidentally, to be a long-time friend of Dean, was ALEC WAUGH who wrote several of his 60 novels here including "Spy in the Family" and "Married to a Spy". Alec was one of the richest British authors Tangier has known although he never flaunted his wealth. On the contrary, he lived quite simply and worked for no pay as Chairman of the Tangier Book Club. He was a familiar sight walking up to the Cafe de Paris every morning with an egg cup in his hand. If that looks odd, don't read back. He carried the egg cup because he liked boiled eggs for breakfast and he found it impossible to persuade the Cafe de Paris to buy some egg cups. Why should they ? Nobody else ordered boiled eggs.

Alec Waugh made half a million dollars from just one of his books. This was "Island in the Sun" which, when filmed, made the singer of the title song world famous. Yes, Harry Belafonte.

During the First War, Alec was captured by the Germans and held in a P.O.W. camp. In WW2 he worked as an Intelligence Officer for the British in Baghdad for three years. Living in Tangier with Alec was his second wife, the talented American novelist Virginia Sorensen. The couple left Tangier five years ago and settled in America where, a few months later, Alec died.

One man who never left Tangier was MORRIS THE MOLE. He was given this nickname because he usually only emerged at night. An intelligent man who spoke nine languages including Russian, Japanese and Arabic, William "Bill" Morris was born in 1911, the son of a draper in Wigan, Lancashire. After taking a First in Classics at Oxford University, he studied Chinese at the School of Oriental Languages in Paris. When the Germans invaded France, Bill was trapped in Paris and, incredibly, using forged identity documents, managed to remain undercover there for the duration of the war.

In 1945 he settled in Tangier and moved into a tiny and cheap back room at the Cecil Hotel. He sometimes ate in restaurants but often made do with tinned sardines or eggs boiled on a camping gas ring next to his toilet. His bible was the British Financial Times which he stacked to the ceiling because he hated to throw anything away.

Most people thought Bill's lifestyle was due to the fact that he was poor and somehow managed to live on a miserly pension. But the miser was Bill. When he died in that Hotel Cecil room in October 1984, his will disclosed that he was worth well over half a million pounds in stocks and shares.

In direct contrast to Bill, the wealthiest Westerner to have lived in Tangier was American multi million heiress, BARBARA HUTTON. To understand her staggering life style it is necessary to mention that at the age of six her Woolworth stores grandfather left her the equivalent of five hundred million Pounds in todays money.

She settled in Tangier in 1946 and bought a house in the Kasbah which she filled with a bonanza of antique furniture worth millions. Shrewdly balancing this opulence, Babs started a soup kitchen to feed some of the needy with free hot soup and bread. Cynics point out that this is an old lurk often employed by the super rich, to get themselves good publicity but also to combat jealousy amongst their immediate neighbours. But, to be charitable, perhaps Babs was being just that ?

In an attempt to enhance her social status in the eyes of Tangier's snobby set, Miss Hutton had a book published, at her own cost, of poems she claimed to have written. Babs always had a hang up about being a shopkeeper's grand daughter and did everything to gain Grace Kelly-style Princess status. She never found herself a King or a world-recognised Prince, but at her fabulous parties in Tangier she sat on a gold throne wearing an emerald and diamond tiara once owned by Empress Catherine of Russia and at her feet were priceless antique silk rugs she had bought from that zillionaire the Shah of Persia.

Barbara Hutton spent thousands of dollars on silk underwear every year but she never had to worry about rinsing out her smalls. After wearing them once, she threw them out. When she felt like a change of scenery, Babs flew to Paris and occupied a luxury suite at the Ritz Hotel. Today, you can rent the same suite for a mere £3,500 a night. While in Morocco she fed her camels on rose petals and when a group of socialites lingered on until dawn at one of her private house parties she walked round dishing out wads of dollars to make them go.

The only thing Babs could not buy was love. She spent her life buying seven husbands and hundreds of young, one-night beach boy lovers. In a desperate attempt to stay young, mega-rich Babs tried plastic surgery and expensive sheep-cell injections. Barbara's critics have described her as a woman whose life was totally wasteful and utterly wasted but many people glimpsed the real tragedy when, just before her death in 1979, the Press carried candid photographs showing her emaciated frame being lifted out of a Rolls Royce in London's Park Lane by a handsome chauffeur. Money, as they say, can't buy everything. Anyone needing proof of this should read the book "Poor Little Rich Girl" by David Heymann (Hutchinson, March 1985).

Going further back into history, the Kasbah home of Barbara Hutton was once owned by another larger than life character. This was WALTER HARRIS, the wealthy son of a British shipping family who was born in 1866 and settled here in 1886. After living in the Kasbah he occupied a mansion on the Malabata side of Tangier which is today the site of the popular Club Med holiday complex.

Although he had rather a playboy attitude towards life in some respects, Harris was not afraid of hard work and acquitted himself well as a correspondent for the British Times newspaper. It has been claimed that he sometimes laced his stories with a dash of fiction to enhance his rather dashing dandy image and some writers have alleged that, using the most popular of all covers, journalism, he was an information gathering agent for the British Government, sometimes under the guise of being a supporter of other regimes. This has never been convincingly proven, but it is known that he did gather political information which he occasionally slipped to various VIP mates which some historians say was rather odd behaviour for a top-drawer Times man, though others put it down to patriotism.

One man who will definitely throw more light on the amazing Walter Harris is James Chandler, a charming British resident of Tangier who has spent many months of deep and dedicated research into the life and times of Harris and is now writing a book on the man.

As a political correspondent, Walter Harris was an important figure in the history of Tangier and he enjoyed many dramatic adventures, including being kidnapped by another incredible character, Ahmed Raisuli, as we shall see in the next two pages, so there is little doubt that James Chandler's book will be made into a film. Walter Harris died in Malta in 1933 and his body was brought back for burial in Tangier's English churchyard of St Andrews where his tombstone still stands today.

FOOTNOTE. *All the characters in this chapter led their own lives and they alone were responsible for their behaviour. No disrespect is intended to any of their innocent relatives, business associates, friends or lovers.*

Tangier's Greatest Rogue

One of the greatest characters in Tangier's history was AHMED RAISULI, also known as "The Sultan of the Mountains", a handsome and intelligent prince of rogues who cocked a snoot at the British and American governments on several occasions. The descendant of a popular Shereef in the Jibala hills near Tangier, Raisuli was a reckless horseman and warrior who led a band of fellow tribesmen, taking what he wanted where and when he wanted it.

He was a combination of a Robin Hood who gave some of his loot to the poor and a Jack the Ripper who chopped the heads or ears off some people who annoyed him. His name was already a legend by the time he was 26 and he was particularly feared by the 6,000 Westerners and 12,000 Moroccans then living in Tangier.

In 1896 Raisuli's foster brother, the Pasha of Tangier, invited him to lunch but before the harira soup was served Raisuli was knocked unconscious by the Pasha's guards. Awaking, he found himself bound in chains and on his way by camel to Mogador where he was thrown in a dungeon. Four long years later he was released along with thousands of other prisoners in a general amnesty. Angry and bitter, Raisuli re-formed his band of rebels and quickly became the most feared man in North West Morocco. Then, in June 1903, he hit on a great idea. He kidnapped WALTER HARRIS, that wealthy English socialite who lived in Tangier and was a correspondent for the Times. Raisuli held Harris in a tatty hut in the hills and Harris was later to relate that his only companion was a headless corpse lying in a corner of the hut. This disciplinary measure put all thought of escape out of Harris's mind and he was a model prisoner.

Raisuli demanded the release of some of his captured followers and he returned Harris to Tangier 20 days later when those comrades were freed. At the time some cynics suspected that Harris had set up his kidnapping in league with Raisuli because, by what might have been an unfortunate coincidence, Raisuli had been a guest at Harris's home prior to the kidnap. Another rumour had it that the British Government had quietly paid a huge ransom for Harris.

In 1904 Raisuli pulled a similar stunt by kidnapping another Tangier socialite, ION PERDICARIS and his stepson, CROMWELL VARLEY. By another coincidence, both happened to be close friends of Walter Harris. Born in 1840 and educated at Harvard, Perdicaris came to Tangier in 1872 where he and his English-born wife, Ellen Varley and her son Cromwell, by a previous marriage, lived in a beautiful mansion which is today the El Minzah Hotel.

Raisuli's snatching of Perdicaris and Varley was sensational because it brought the two super powers, Britain and America into the picture. As a former Harvard man, Perdicaris was regarded as American as apple pie and his stepson Cromwell, of course, was a British subject. In return for their release Raisuli demanded an astonishing four-pronged ransom.

First, he wanted 70,000 dollars in cash. Second, the release of yet more of his captured followers being held in Tangier's Kasbah jail. Third, he wanted the imprisonment of various men he named as his enemies. The fourth and most audacious demand, and Raisuli insisted on this, was that he be appointed Governor of all districts round Tangier.

These diabolical demands threw the British and American governments into fits of rage and the case became world news. President THEODORE ROOSEVELT sent no less than seven American warships to Tangier with a multitude of marines armed to the teeth and raring to fight. This fleet was quickly joined by a group of equally armed British warships sent from Gibraltar. In typical media-manipulating style, Roosevelt arranged for "Harpers Weekly" magazine to run a tub-thumping story which boasted that the American fleet would "bombard or occupy not only Tangier, but every port in Morocco".

A little later, Roosevelt's tough Secretary of State, JOHN HAY, sent a cable which read in part : "This government wants Perdicaris alive or Raisuli dead". All this could easily have ruined Roosevelt's political career because, hilariously, Ion Perdicaris was not the American citizen everyone thought.

Some 42 years earlier he had quietly taken out Greek nationality because he had, in fact, been born in Athens. This meant that Roosevelt had wrongly embarked on a big flag flying exercise which not only wrongly interfered in the domestic policies of a foreign country, but wrongly involved all those American warships full of marines in a provocative war situation and wrongly demanded the death of a Moroccan citizen, Raisuli -- all for a Greek .

But shrewdy Roosevelt, when he was informed of this, ordered that it be kept top secret and the truth only leaked out 29 years later in 1933 when nobody really cared. In the end, after 37 days of wasted wrangling and world headlines, all opposition to Raisuli collapsed. He was paid the ransom and his jailed comrades were released.

Secretary of State John Hay got a medal, in spite of that undiplomatic telegram, and Roosevelt was re-elected that November by a huge majority of votes. That, as they say, is showbiz. But Raisuli didn't care about all this political nonsense. He knew he had beaten the infidels. He had his jailed colleagues safely back in his camp, he had all that ransom money, several of his enemies were quietly jailed or told to vanish and, as a cherry on top, Raisuli was, as he had insisted, appointed the Governor of North West Morocco.

The biggest loser was Ion Perdicaris. Running scared, he sold up in Tangier and, with his wife, Ellen, retired to a quieter life in a luxury mansion nestling in the green and more tranquil English meadows of Tunbridge Wells.

In 1907, Raisuli pulled yet another fast one by kidnapping Scots-born Tangier resident HARRY "CAID" MACLEAN, the son of a British Army General. He was important in the eyes of Whitehall because his job in Morocco was Chief Instructor to the Shereefian Army and this made him extremely valuable for the British political machine. Some historians claim Harry was another secret agent for the British but whether this was true or not, Raisuli decided he was worth a 100,000 dollar ransom. That's what he demanded. He also wanted to be instated as the Governor of all Northern Morocco. Third, and most cunning of all, he insisted that he be made a British protected subject which would insure him against being arrested or jailed. In return for all this, he said he would stop his kidnapping nonsense.

The British Government said it would never agree to such a humiliating deal. Never. So Raisuli held on to Harry Maclean and said he would never be released. Never. Seven long months later the British knuckled under and Raisuli won yet again. He got the money, he was appointed Governor of all Northern Morocco and he became a fully protected British protège.

Harry Maclean returned to his instructing work for the local army and became Inspector General. Later, he was decorated at Buckingham Palace and became Sir Harry. A Tangier street was named after him and so was Caid's Bar in the basement of the El Minzah Hotel where his portrait by Irishman John Lavery still hangs today.

Raisuli, who went on to work as an agent for the Germans in World War One, seems to have met several suspected or actual British agents. Another was an English authoress who wrote under the name ROSITA

FORBES. Her real name however was McGrath and she was married to Colonel Arthur McGrath who just happened to work for the British War Office. In 1923, Rosita came to Tangier on a secret mission for her husband which was to talk to Raisuli at his hillside hideout at Zinat where he had again decided to operate as a roaming bandit. It would appear that Rosita was bowled over by the handsome rogue for she stayed as his guest for two weeks and then returned home to write a book about his life. Entitled "The Sultan of the Mountains" it was published in New York the following year.

Raisuli, who had taken on and mastered not only the British, Americans and various Governors was, in the end, beaten in battle by his own people in January 1925. His men were wiped out and he was banished to the village of Tamasint where he died peacefully of natural causes three months later. The old fox had the last laugh though. When servants went to burn the straw packed mattress he had died on they heard a strange clanking noise. Inside, they found a fortune in gold coins and jewels along with various documents which are now exhibited in the museum of his old castle at Asilah.

The legend of Ahmed Raisuli lives on and there's still a great film to be made about his life. In the Seventies, a film was made but it was farcical in terms of representing the man. Entitled "The Wind and the Lion" that James Bonder Sean Connery played the role of Raisuli and he was good. But, in typical Hollywood style, real life history was changed to bring a bit of sex into it, wouldn't you guess ? Instead of kidnapping Ion Perdicaris, the movie moguls made it Mrs Perdicaris who was abducted and that lady's role was performed by Candice Bergen.

A Tempting Spook

The veiled lady above is a ghost. Her name is AISHA KANDISHA. Many regard her as something of a heroine but others see her as a devil or an object of pity. Yet whatever view is taken, nobody denies she's a fascinating character. If you doubt this, mention her name to any male Moroccan and he will, after registering initial surprise that you know her name, launch into a lengthy explanation.

The story differs from man to man because Aisha is a contradictory lady but the basic details are that she is a sensuous woman who lusts after all men and tries to tempt them with her beauty. No woman has ever set eyes on this femme fatale, which almost certainly explains why she is reputed to be ravishingly attractive with a delectable figure and an intense aura of carnal knowledge in her piercing brown eyes.

Aisha's favourite haunts are at the main entrance gate to the Tangier Kasbah; along the road near the de luxe Malabata Hotel and by the Jew's River below the Marshan. She usually wears a glittering silver djellabah of fine silk which is rather transparent and she walks with such grace that many say she seems to float. Although she has a marked preference for Moroccans she sometimes materialises before tourists, particularly if they have been watching belly dancers, who apparently arouse her jealousy.

Strangely, the lady ghost seems to know some of her victims. Dozens of witnesses have affirmed that she called out their full name as she beckoned them with her fingers. Most of the men who have seen her insist that Aisha appeared to be quite real until she screamed and melted away before their eyes.

A couple of tourists have confessed that they ran to the nearest bar to drink themselves silly after meeting Aisha. This has led to a cunning anti-Aisha smear campaign which alleges that only drunkards see her. But one eminently respectable Tangier businessman, who was and is a tee-totaller, was so shocked that he lost his voice and hearing for three months after seeing the lady ghost in 1974 when he was aged 28. He only recovered his voice and hearing after being exorcised by a local man of religion.

Many Moroccans believe Aisha was a promiscuous woman, now in limbo, who has been unable to cleanse her soul of man's evil and finds it impossible to enter into Gloria (Heaven). There is another legend about Aisha which claims that when she meets a man of really bad character she disturbs his mind so that he is unable to live a normal life thereafter. Any good man who allows Aisha to embrace him is said to be rewarded with a gift of diamonds, though no man has ever come forward with proof of this in the form of gems. Maybe they were worried that the Tax Man might want to take a cut.

It is rumoured that the bewitching siren has the cloven hooves of a goat which are mostly hidden by her long djellabah, but super shrewd Moroccans counter this claim by saying it is a lie invented by women in a desperate attempt to reduce Aisha's sex appeal to their menfolk.

Westerners who have not seen Aisha are entitled to scoff at her legend but most Moroccans point to the fact that she has been seen far too many times for reasonable doubt to be entertained and the widespread belief in Aisha is such that an Italian company has made a full-length film based on her exploits.

HISTORICAL FOOTNOTE. *The Finnish anthropologist, EDWARD WESTERMARCK, who specialised in Moroccan folklore, links Aisa Quandisa (his spelling) to Astarte, the ancient goddess of fertility, suggesting she may have originated with the Carthagenian colonies of Northern Morocco, which would make Aisha just about as ancient as Tangier. See Westermarck's book "Ritual and Belief in Morocco,, London 1926, Volume One, Pages 392 onwards.*

Characters You

May Meet

People often sigh nostalgically about the great characters of the good old days. ''There just aren't any left'' they complain. But they are wrong. Tangier is home to many fascinating personalities.

Of the British crowd here, JOHN SUTCLIFFE is probably the easiest to approach. Most nights he can be found at the curved bar of the Tanger Inn. That's the local English pub, not to be confused with the Tangier Hotel. The Tanger Inn pub only opens at 9pm but it is a popular rendezvous for many British residents as well as tourists. Based in the Rue Magellan it nestles on a hill between the seafront Cecil Hotel and the Rembrandt Hotel at the start of Boulevard Pasteur. If you are going there at night for the first time it's perhaps better to take a taxi.

The Tanger Inn is a mixture of night spot and local pub, though they do not have draught beer, where dress is casual and music is played quietly as background or a bit louder when there's a crowd dancing. They have a baby grand piano for any guest who wants to play it.

There's no better place for tourists wanting to learn what makes Tangier tick and even the shyest person, male or female, whether accompanied or not, can be sure of a warm welcome. All you have to do is walk up to the bar and ask for John Sutcliffe or Peter Tuckwell, who started the bar in 1965. Instant and interesting conversation is guaranteed as both men know Tangier backwards and, if you are an interesting person, you will find yourself being introduced to other customers. This is one of the great charms of the Tanger Inn as most tourists are keen to communicate with Tangier locals.

You might be told the Tanger Inn is a "gay" bar yet, while it is true that several gay British residents like the sophisticated and often slick chatter at the bar, the place is more often gay in another sense. One night you might find half the bar stools occupied by rich American matrons competing with each other to buy drinks. Another night you might have to force your way through a dance floor milling with couples from Yorkshire doing a Knees Up Mother Brown.

The Tanger Inn has a very varied clientèle but the two owners are quite different. PETER TUCKWELL is a languid charmer capable of quick quips which he uses to cover up a rather shy nature.

By contrast, John Sutcliffe is a born raconteur who has some great yarns to tell. Born in Huddersfield, John has enjoyed a very full life. Everyone in Tangier knows he is a former actor, painter and BBC broadcaster, but few know he was held in a Japanese prisoner of war camp during WW2. You will be lucky, however, if you get him to talk about his camp experiences which were traumatic and contributed to the break up of his marriage.

In his early youth John was a trooper in the Household Cavalry and later a Captain in the Indian Army. After the war he became public relations officer for London's Westminster Council and in 1963 ended up being head of the Local Government Information Office for the whole of England and Wales.

A chameleon of a character, John has a Doctorate in Philosophy and writes in his spare time. Apart from many poems and feature articles for newspapers, he is the author of "Unknown Pilgrim" an unusual story of a young man who, as an act of atonement, walks barefoot from Tangier to Northern Ireland and performs several miracles on the way. A British company is now planning to make a film of the book. In between acting and journalism John was once, wait for it, a daily server at Mass in Westminster Cathedral. This probably explains why, in the absence of clergy, the local British community has twice called upon John to officiate at burial proceedings in Tangier.

Above the Tanger Inn bar is the homely El Muniria Hotel which is run by Peter Tuckwell and his managing director, ABDUL JYOU. Single rooms cost about £4 nightly. Many famous people have stayed there and Americans might be interested to know that William Burroughs, the Harvard educated grandson of the adding machine millionaire made his name by writing his confessional drug scene novel "Naked Lunch" in Room nine. Lunch being heroin.

AIME SERFATY of the highly popular Rif Hotel is definitely a success story. He started working at the Rif as a temporary and junior receptionist paid no wage in 1946. Today he is the co-owner. Born in Fez, the son of a prominent businessman, Aime enjoyed a good education and studied law after leaving school but law did not suit his personality so he decided to try his luck in America and travelled up to Tangier with the intention of working his way to New York on a cargo boat. While waiting for his ship to arrive he ran out of money and started feeling hungry. Rather than ask his father for funds he walked into the Rif and asked for a temporary job. After a little haggling the manager hired him, but without a wage. All he got was two meals a day. When the time came for Aime to board that boat to America the Rif Manager realised he risked losing a good worker and tempted him with a full-time job at a wage of £5 a month plus two daily meals and a small room in the hotel.

As he accepted, Aime promised himself he would take one of those boats to America eventually. But fate decided otherwise. Working at the Rif was so interesting for Aime that he threw himself into the job heart and soul, which is a sure fire recipe for success. Two years later he was rewarded by being promoted to head receptionist. In 1950 he was made assistant manager and manager three years later. Today, Aime Serfaty is not just the co-owner of the Rif. He's also the General Manager of the Solazur Hotel and in addition runs the splendid Tariq Hotel on the Malabata side of Tangier Bay. He is a rarity in Tangier insofar that his full-time private secretary is English. A charming lady from the North of England, Margaret has lived in Tangier for over ten years and gives that little extra British flavour to the Rif.

Nobody understands British tourists better than Aime Serfaty. He speaks English fluently as well as four other languages and his ability to recognise honeymoon couples who return for a secret anniversary is legend at the Rif. Although he is known to be one of the toughest operators in the hotel trade when it comes to buying and bargaining, Aime can let his hair down when he feels like it. Anyone who doubts this should see him stand at the Rif bar telling jokes.

We watched him do this for an hour one lunchtime and he kept the whole bar in fits of laughter. The best part is that Aime was clever enough to make himself the "fall" guy in many of his jokes. When he tells a story about his marriage, to an attractive Frenchwoman, his wife always emerges as the winner.

Aime has many funny stories to tell about his career at the Rif, but you will never hear him mention the name of any guest who might have been involved in some indiscretion. He's far too diplomatic for that. He is, however, proud of the fact that many world-famous people have stayed there and he remembers which rooms they occupied. Testing him, we asked which room Winston Churchill had occupied with Clementine in 1958. As quick as a flash came the answer. Room 520. Yes, Aime Serfaty is a character. This was confirmed in January 1985 when he was named in Tangier's Merit List as a Citizen of Honour and Distinction.

Other citizens of distinction in Tangier include members of the local ROTARY CLUB which meets at the Rif Hotel every Tuesday night. Visiting Rotarians are welcome to introduce themselves.

Another weekly event at the Rif is their free FASHION SHOW which is great fun for all ages because about 15 holidaying couples are enlisted to act as models.

The ladies wear caftans in beautiful colours with intricately embroidered gold or silver necklines. For ladies, the modelling is serious and elegant but for their husbands or boy friends it's a giggle to wear those baggy trousers or long, striped djellabahs with a fez perched on their heads. The show usually starts at 10pm and guests from other hotels are welcome to attend this fun evening free of any entrance charge. Don't be shy about volunteering as models. Anyone can do it, even tiny tots, and the photographs of you parading round the dance floor make great conversation pieces when you return home. Apply to the Entertainments Manager at the Rif on the day before the show. Don't worry about the garments. They are new and provided free. Women have at least 100 to choose from.

One entertainment not put on by the Rif but which happens on the shoreline opposite the hotel is a little family fishing business run by MOHAMED BEN MOUSSA and his son Ali, aged 21. Between 6 and 9 several mornings a week you will see them trawling for fish with a large black inner tube and a fine muslin-ended net. If you have children, take them to watch these men in action. As an object lesson about the work ethic, it's most educational. Called Changuettes, the fish they catch are so matchstick small that it all seems to be a waste of time.

But their hard labour reaps them about 15 kilos which is sold to restaurants for making delicious fish soup and omelettes.

Package holiday tourists arriving in Tangier have a travel firm representative to turn to for advice and these reps are usually interesting characters and the great pity is that some of them only stay here for brief spells of duty.

Still with the ladies we have EMMA BODENZ who was born in Holland and came to Tangier in 1951 to open, of all things, a pickled herring factory. A few years later she and her brother Harry decided to set up a taxi company in this city. They called it Chico Taxi because they pioneered the use of small cars all equipped with radio receivers. Within months, London firms pinched the idea and that is how mini cabs were born which upset London's Hackney cab drivers somewhat and started that famous mini cab war.

She's a very capable lady is Emma. Determined too. When she started the taxi firm it was necessary for her to obtain a local driving licence. All other Western women driving cars here at that time did so on International Driving Permits etc, but for Emma to drive a vehicle for hire was a different matter and turned out to be something of a problem. For some strange reason she failed on taking the local driving test so she took it again. And failed again. On taking the test a third time she made it her business to find out why she had failed. The answer was simple. There were no Moroccan women drivers here in those days. Such a thing was unthinkable in this man's man's world. And that's why the French authorities, not surprisingly, could not find the right form for her to fill in and solved the problem by failing her. In the end, after some hair-tearing, Emma got her local licence. The very first woman in Morocco to get one, which is a sweet bit of history.

Today, you will find Emma running the Beach Bar Caroussel (BBC) on the beachfront opposite the Miramar Hotel. She's easy to recognise as she usually wears a white safari suit. She is Mine Host par excellence if she likes the look of you but, if you are one of those chaps who snaps his fingers to catch a waiter's attention, watch out : Emma can deliver a blistering mouthful when annoyed. After you have been to Emma's a couple of times don't be surprised if she showers you with free chunks of her homemade English cake for which she is quite famed. All the food at Emma's is good but her fish dishes, with classic British chips, are most popular with English tourists.

Emma Bodenz has led a most interesting life, particularly as a young girl in Europe during the war. BRIAN DESMOND HURST, a famous British film director who once lived in this city, begged her to write a book, assuring her it would make a great film. Emma has agreed to tape her wartime experiences but insists the story should only be disclosed after her death. The person entrusted with these tapes is JOAN PEARSON, another Tangier character. Born in Yorkshire, Joan has visited this town every summer since 1968 and most afternoons she is to be found sitting at the corner table inside Emma's bar where many British residents pop in for a beer and catch up with all the gossip.

Another character worth a book is Welshman TONY WILLIAMS, the Tangier rep for Columbia Films. On leaving school he worked as a trainee for the Midland Bank in Cardiff but, tiring of counting other people's money, he ran off to London at the age of 20 and, having a fine tenor voice, took singing lessons from Ivor Novello's mother.

After landing a singing role in The Merry Widow, his theatrical career was interrupted by Hitler. Joining the RAF he carried out several hair-raising missions over Germany as the rear gunner in a Lancaster bomber and was then transferred to South Africa where, on approaching Durban harbour, his troopship was torpedoed.

After the war, which claimed the lives of his three elder brothers, all airmen, Tony continued his showbiz career and in the Fifties, doubled for Laurence Olivier in five major films including "The Prince and the Showgirl" with Marilyn Monroe. In 1957 Olivier urged Tony to better himself by going into film production and, to help him in this, gave him a personal intro to the senior director of Columbia Films in Britain who appointed him as Columbia's man in Morocco.

During the next 25 years Tony did all the groundwork for many films made or partly made in Morocco. One of the best was 'Young-Winston' starring Simon Ward and Robert Shaw. Another was 'Hard Contract' starring Lee Remick, Lily Palmer and James Coburn. Tony could make a lot of money writing gossip stories about some of the stars. During the filming of one epic, the wife of the world famous male lead ran off to the Rif Mountains for a month with a handsome young Moroccan. She enjoyed herself so much that she took the young chap back to America, despite hubby's protests.

When Tony arranged the filming of "Dubious Patriots" in 1970, Tony Curtis and Charles Bronson hated each other so much that they refused to speak to each other off set. Not all the films were successful and some never reached the screen although a million dollars had been spent on them in Morocco.

On one occasion Tony had to build a complete village of stone and wood dwellings with Roman-style pillars and walls all round. Not just that. The film men wanted the village to be in a remote valley outside Marrakech. This took several months and was for "The Man Who Would Be King", in which Sean Connery and Michael Caine were often eclipsed by the brilliant Moroccan actor LARBI DOGHMI whose tremendous performance made him an overnight success.

Tony Williams has some fascinating memories. Marilyn Monroe cried on his shoulders several times in London because she felt insecure acting alongside Laurence Olivier and kept forgetting her lines. She also cried because her egg head husband, American dramatist Arthur Miller, hated the British and kept saying so. Five years ago, Bette Davis chose Tony to accompany her to Russia where she intended financing a film and he speaks highly of Bette. Another good friend was Diana Dors who was planning to stay at Tony's beautiful 300 year old home in the Kasbah until she lost her brave battle against cancer in 1984.

Another showbiz name is PAUL DANQUAH, a charismatic Tangier resident who achieved fame in Britain when he played the role of Jimmy the seaman in the controversial 1960 film "A Taste of Honey." Controversial because, in the film, Jimmy was a Coloured man who had an affair with Persil-white Rita Tushingham and made her pregnant. Quite shocking indeed in those uptight days according to the Fleet Street film critics and guardians of public morals who said the inter-racial sex theme of the film was "Kitchen sink" and "mucky". The criticism didn't worry Paul though because he's not the ordinary run of the mill actor.

Born in London in 1925, his mother was English, his maternal grandmother Irish and his father was Dr J.B. Danquah, the distinguished lawyer and leader of the Opposition in Ghana who died in a political prison while detained by the Kwame Nkrumah regime. Educated in Britain, Paul followed his father's footsteps by studying law and becoming a barrister when he was called to the British Bar in 1958. As a law student, Paul earned pocket money by doing religious and children's programmes for the BBC. He says he was only flirting with the acting profession but still ended up making that name for himself in "A Taste of Honey" and later grabbed plum roles in the TV series "Danger Man" and "The Avengers".

Towards the end of WW2, Paul served in the Medical Corps in Italy and Greece. He says he gave up acting because he didn't have the courage to cope with the lean days actors suffer but have to pretend they are "resting" in order to keep up appearances. Instead, after making the thriller film "Maroc Zero Seven" on location in Tangier in 1968, Paul accepted the prestige job as a senior information officer for the World Bank. Based in Washington DC, he spent the next 15 years producing and broadcasting radio programmes for overseas distribution.

A talented amateur pianist and singer, Paul settled in Tangier in 1983 although he had been visiting this city yearly since 1955. Still a consultant for the World Bank and a director of a Tangier building company, he lives in a pretty villa on the Charf. That's the select hillside area topped with fir trees behind the Solazur Hotel.

Another well-known personality is local landowner, MALCOM S. FORBES, a distinguished art collector, expert balloonist, motorbike enthusiast and publisher of the prestige "Forbes" business magazine which, in 1975, introduced a popular Arabic edition. Malcolm Forbes bought the Mendoub Tazi's palace in Rue Shakespeare, Marshan, and turned it into a unique and impressive museum of military miniatures which any tourist can visit free of charge, courtesy of Forbes Magazine.

The rare and valuable toy soldiers on show in large glass cases are a must for ex-servicemen, war historians and youngsters.

As a Staff Sergeant in WW2, Malcolm was wounded in action and awarded the Bronze Star. In 1973 he became the first to cross the United States in a hot air balloon and broke six world records doing so. A constant world traveller, married with five children, Malcolm Forbes throws entertaining parties when in Tangier. Although he is a successful and serious-minded tycoon, and a working Editor, he has a great sense of humour and has written a cute business advice book wittily entitled "The Sayings of Chairman Malcolm" as well as another business book, "Fact and Comment".

The late American Senator, Hubert Humphrey, once called Malcolm Forbes the "Bob Hope of business publications". Whether that remark was meant kindly or not doesn't matter because Malcolm is man enough to poke fun at himself as is evidenced by the private aircraft he bought in the Seventies. He had it painted gold and named it "Capitalist Tool." With a sense of humour like that, we wish him many happy landings.

A different American living in Tangier is New York-born artist ROBERT BARNETE who settled here after spending 28 years in Spain where he was Knighted for his services to Spanish art.

Robert is well worth meeting as he is a highly intelligent man of great charm who mixes easily with people from all walks of life and to listen to him talk about Morocco is very rewarding. Apart from being a brilliant lateral thinker, Robert has taken the trouble to get to know Moroccans at first hand. By living with them in the deserts and mountains but, more important, by learning their language, even the various dialects.

Robert can paint anything from Flamenco dancers to Kasbah scenes but today he specialises in spectacular Arabian horses and robed riders. HRH King Fahd of Saudi Arabia recently bought 20 of Robert's paintings for the walls of his beautiful Tangier Palace. Other proud owners are the Moroccan King, HRH Moulay Hassan II ; the King of Cambodia ; the Maharaja of Jaipur and Henry Kissinger.

Robert's paintings are available from famous galleries in Casablanca, London, Paris and Madrid, but there's nothing to stop you contacting him directly by telephone at his Tangier home. If you wish to see examples of his work there's one on a large easel in the reception area of the Rif Hotel. Another is on an easel opposite Fatima's little boutique on the mezzanine floor of the El Minzah Hotel.

Inside Fatima's boutique you will also find work by Tangier-born HAMID BARNOUSSI, who lives in the Kasbah. He produces delicate and sensitive pastels of typical local scenes. Well worth considering if you are a small collector.

OLGA BENCHEKROUN, the wife of the Honorary Portuguese Consul, is another artist. Experts have described her pastels and oils as having a rare touch of genius, particularly her Portuguese landscapes which, quite naturally, can be seen hanging on the walls of the Portuguese Consulate.

Another talented lady is British-born PATRICIA HASKINS who settled here in 1963 after a successful career as an advertising and fashion artist in London and Paris. An exhibition of her fine works was held in the Old American Legation recently and, writing about it in the local Dépêche de Tanger, Britisher Patrick Thursfield stated that he would like to see more. We agree.

Four other excellent artists are Swedish-born ELSA TORNA-HIELM, whose 'snowflake' effect pastels can be seen in the lounge of the El Minzah ; British-born MURIEL PHILLIPS, whose paintings hang in the foyer of the Tanjah Flandria Hotel ; LINDA ARMS-TRONG, a vivacious American at present back in the States and her talented daughter Salowa, aged 19, who drew the clever sketches for this book.

Back to the men we have Tangier's own MOHAMED HAMRI whose oils, pastels and pen and ink drawings are all the more awe inspiring when you know he is self taught. A versatile man, he helped the Rolling Stones to re-create the sacred song, 'Pipes of Pan' and the British born author Brion Gyson has written a book about him entitled 'The Process'. Mohamed is married to Blanca, a personality plus American from Coney Island who works at the American School of Tangier as the headmaster's private secretary.

No Tangier book would be complete without a mention of PAUL BOWLES, an American author who first came here in 1931 at the age of

21. Paul's books on Morocco and his translations from Arabic are a must for serious students of the Moroccan way of life.

In addition to being a writer, Paul is a talented musician who has adapted Jean Paul Sartre's work for the theatre. He also wrote the scores for Broadway hits such as "Cyrano de Bergerac".

In the Fifties, Paul and his delightful wife, Jane, were the undisputed leaders of the local avant-garde set. Jane has been described by American playwright Tennessee Williams as "the greatest writer of our century in the English language" and in this judgement he was supported by Harold Pinter. But the world was cruelly robbed of Jane's talents when she suffered a stroke, leading to an early death in 1973. Paul Bowles' autobiography, "Without Stopping", (1972) makes interesting reading and explains his friendships with a wide variety of world-famous personalities.

During the early stages of World War Two, American Intelligence feared that the German juggernaut might occupy the strategic areas of Morocco, Algeria and Tunisia, so it recruited several trusted Americans who had knowledge of these countries.

GORDON BROWNE, a Boston tea broker who had studied anthropology at Harvard, was one of the ones chosen for Morocco because he knew the country well and had some dependable friends here. Operating under State Department cover he, along with eleven other Americans who became known as "The Twelve Apostles", worked for General William "Wild Bill" Donovan's crack Office of Strategic Services (O.S.S.) and busied themselves gathering intelligence and operational information.

Gordon Browne was mainly based in Tangier and enjoyed a friendly working relationship with Britain's Secret Operations Executive (SOE). He saw combat as a civilian while running the secret radio beacon "Rebecca" outside Oran, Algeria. Rebecca was a British invention which Browne used to guide in the American paratroopers flying in from England on 7 November 1942, as part of the famous Anglo-American "Torch" invasion.

Mention any of this to Gordon Browne, as we did, and he will almost certainly brush it off by saying : "That was all a long time ago" and then he will adroitly change the subject. Yes, he's a modest fellow, but the Rogue's Guide isn't going to let him get away with it. One fact he cannot dismiss is that he was awarded the Presidential Medal for Merit by Franklin D. Roosevelt for his bravery in the "Torch" invasion campaign during which he attacked and silenced an enemy machine gun post single-handed. For this snippet we are grateful to the famous American anthropologist, CARLETON S. COON.

Professor Coon was another American agent who operated in Tangier and thanks to him we can also relate the following true spy story. During the war, he and Gordon Browne were asked by British Intelligence to make a trip through French Morocco and gather typical stones they found along the country roads.

The idea was that London would make copies of the stones filled with explosives and these would be laid along strategic roads to blow up enemy troop convoys in the event of an invasion.

Driving along the roads they found few stones but did notice an abundance of mule turds. Turning to Carleton Coon, Browne suggested they should send samples of these turds to London in the British Diplomatic Bag, along with the suggestion that they be copied. Whitehall thought this was a great idea and approved the scheme. And that is the story behind the Browne-Coon "Mule Turd" landmines which were used effectively against the Germans in Tunisia and Italy. Today, Gordon Browne and his charming wife Eleanor live in vigorous retirement at their Spanish type villa on the Marshan.

Another American veteran of Tangier is California-born ANNE HARBACH who only intended to stay here one week when she first came in 1956 to spend a holiday in the Kasbah home of the talented Canadian painter, CHRISTOPHER WANKLYN. Anne is the granddaughter of Edwin T. Earl, the California newspaper tycoon whose long term support put Teddy Roosevelt into the White House in 1901.

A nursing aide during WW2, Anne was married to the late Robert Harbach who worked as a desk man for the CIA in Washington. He was the son of Otto Harbach, the lyricist who wrote 'Desert Song', 'Rose Marie', 'No,No, Nanette' and 49 other world famous songs. Of independent means, Anne Harbach is a sophisticated lady who has a seemingly inexhaustible fund of entertaining anecdotes and stories to tell about Tangier. Most days, Anne can be seen lunching at the Nautilus Restaurant or at Emma's BBC beach bar during summer afternoons.

Another regular at Emma's is DON COLLINS, a former antique dealer in Britain and Gibraltar whose hobbies include gardening, writing poetry, designing exquisite jewellery or pottering about on his 72-foot yacht, Aquarine.

Another Tangier resident who loves the sea is ANNA MCKEW, a former South African socialite and champion water skier who, before she decided to settle in this city, was a very popular beauty in London's chic and trendy Chelsea Set. Today she lives in an elegantly furnished villa on the Marshan overlooking the Straits of Gibraltar.

A Brief, for the British, History

"Tangier is the richest jewel in my crown", said KING CHARLES THE SECOND of Britain and Ireland in 1661 when he was given the city as a wedding present on the occasion of his marriage to the Portuguese Princess, CATHERINE OF BRAGANZA. She, by the way, was responsible for making tea-drinking highly fashionable in England. Say a big thank you Messrs Brooke Bond, Lyons, Liptons and Tetley.

Historians tell us that Charlie Two did not love Catherine but wed her because Tangier was really what he lusted after.

This makes sense when you read Antonia Fraser's excellent book "Charles II" in which she discloses that Charlie actually loved Barbara Palmer who was the "uncrowned Queen of England" and had five children by her whereas he had none by curvaceous Catherine. We can't criticise Charlie for marrying Catherine though. The Portuguese gave him well over a quarter of a million Pounds as a dowry and threw in Tangier and Bombay as extras.

The wily Portuguese conned Charlie with Tangier. It was a very hot political potato and under regular seige by Sultan Moulay Ismail's followers. To keep these chaps down King Charles sent 27 ships carrying 3,000 British troops to Tangier. Led by LORD PETERBOROUGH, the troops landed at Tangier's port in January 1662 and quickly discovered that the Portuguese had taken with them the doors, windows and wooden floors of nearly all the decent houses. Lord Peterborough grabbed the former Portuguese Governor's Palace in the Kasbah as his little pad while the lower ranks lived in tents like genuine Bedouin. Then Peterborough tidied up the town by destroying most of the buildings of religion not agreeing with King Charlie's which upset the locals somewhat and made them just that little bit more rebellious.

Three months later, on 3 May 1662, some 500 Britsh troops led by a Colonel Fines, ventured out of the garrison and headed towards the Old Mountain a couple of miles away.

Before getting there they were cleverly ambushed by Moulay Ismail's men and wiped out. Charles Two then sent Scots-born Big Bill Rutherford, known as the EARL OF TEVIOT, to Tangier. British historians tell us that Teviot quickly won the respect of the local population with his "personal gallantry and charm" but local historians tell rather a different story. They affirm that only the local shopkeepers liked Teviot and that he was so scared of the rebellious Moors that he cuddled a musket and sword in bed with him every night. History doesn't bother to tell us whether this shot his wife's nerves to pieces or cut her to the quick.

What we do know is that eventually the Whitehall nabobs ordered the Earl to leave his heavily fortified fort and rope in, by the neck no doubt, a few of those unruly Moors known to be agitating among the populace on the outskirts of Tangier. With a heavy heart and surrounded by no less than 500 heavily armed troops, our brave and beloved Earl, carrying a rifle, two hand guns, a sword and a dagger, ventured out of his fort on 3 May 1664. He should have known better. The choice of that date was ridiculous. It was two years to the day since Colonel Fines and his 500 had been wiped out after daring to leave the Fort. Tempting coincidence even further the foolhardy Earl Teviot actually led his 500 troops along exactly the same route towards the Old Mountain where Moulay Ismail's highly organised force ambushed him and his 500 and cut them to ribbons.

Only nine English troops survived, which was convenient for King Charlie and his Royal Treasury because it is an historical fact that when they died, the 491 soldiers were all owed two years back pay. In fact, things were so bad in the British garrison at the time that all the shovels in the fort had secretly been sold by the British privates, which is another historical fact and perhaps explains why the bodies of all those 491 troops, with the exception of Earl Teviot of course, were left to rot where they lay instead of being given a decent burial.

As can be seen, it was not much fun being a British private in those days. In fact, all lower ranks were held in a tight grip with vicious punishment being meted out if they stepped out of line. Have one too many jugs of beer and you were placed in the stocks for public ridicule, with the officers egging on the sergeants to throw rotten fruit in your face. Try to desert or steal anything worth more than one shilling and you were shot. This might explain the loss of all those shovels which, in those days, were worth only tuppence. Several British soldiers who whispered that the Muslim religion was superior to ours were placed in chains and had holes drilled in their tongues with a white-hot poker. This may sound incredible but it's horrible fact.

In 1680 the British suffered another major blow when rebels ambushed and killed 119 officers and troops. Their heads were stuck on staves and placed round the outer garrison walls as a little progaganda lesson to the Englishmen inside. Slowly but painfully it became clear to King Charles that Tangier was not worth all the hassle, quite apart from the fact that manning the city cost him 13 per cent of England's total annual income even if he forgot about the astronomical cost (two million over 15 years) of building the harbour mole which was done by two English engineers, Mr HENRY SHERE and SIR HUGH CHOLMLEY, who also built the famous mole at Whitby.

Most history books tell how the British evacuated Tangier in 1684, but few bother to explain exactly why, before leaving, they destroyed that lovely long and curved mole. Some historians say the Brits blew up the mole. Not true. About 2,000 British soldiers demolished it with sledge hammers over a period of three months. They did however, blow up Yorke Castle on the Kasbah hillside and several other forts. The explosion at Yorke Castle being captured on canvas by WINCESLAUS HOLLER, King Charlie's favourite painter. All this destruction was masterminded by Charlie's special agent Mr SAMUEL PEPYS. This is the famous Pepys who was MP for Harwich in 1697, Secretary to the Admiralty in 1684 and who is renowned (a cunning media term meaning we like him) for the 3,000 page, six volumed Diary he kept. The Diary, of course, gives rather a different account of his days in this city where he was appointed Treasurer in 1665. Even today, relatively few people know that the world was conned by the early editors of Pepys' Diary, who suppressed much of the villainy in it. The reason being to hide from the masses the fact that such an illustrious member of the Upper Class could be such a villain. The truth came out however in 1899, for the few who could read in those days, when an honest scribe named H.B. WHEATLEY, in his exposé of the Pepys Diary, entitled "Pepysiana" included material in which Samuel Pepys, by his own written words, was proved to be licentious in thought and deed, an unfaithful husband, a seducer and a rogue who lined his pockets while he was King's Treasurer here. Slippery Sam swiped a hefty commission from most of the monies Charlie Two sent to his city. Pepys was arrested and jailed in Tangier on charges of fraud but managed to slip money bribes here there and everywhere to buy himself out of trouble as he did later in England when he was, on different charges, arrested and held in the Tower of London.

You will find no mention whatsoever of all this chicanery in your children's history books or school books. Samuel Pepys is still presented to the masses as some kind of saint and his former London lodgings bear a commemorative plaque and various establishments are named in his honour as well as two roads, one street and one crescent.

Credit where it's due though. Samuel Pepys would have made a great scandal reporter for Fleet Street's sexy Sundays. In his Diary he includes many tit bits of gossip about life in Tangier. The most titillating being, perhaps, his recording of the fact that in the short space of one month, thirty days to be precise, a girl named Joyce had sold her favours to no less than 400 of the British troops based in the Tangier garrison and that all 400 had to be treated for pox. Joyful Joyce really was a busybody but you will find no mention of her astonishing record in the Guinness Book of.

Another famous Englishman who came to Tangier was HORATIO NELSON who arrived in October 1805 when his fleet ran out of money and provisions. He couldn't have liked Tangier because he spent much of his time sitting in the quarterdeck suite of his flagship "Victory" writing letters of love. Not to his wife, Fanny, but to his mistress EMMA HAMILTON who bore his illegitimate girl child, Horatia.

As Nelson sat writing, one of his men dashed round Tangier trying to cadge money. It was no easy task as you can imagine if you have been here longer than two hours, but finally a local named MOSES PARIENTE took a gamble and lent several thousand Pounds on the strength of an IOU simply signed "Nelson".

Using the money, our brave admiral sailed off to Gibraltar to buy food and cannonballs which helped him to defeat a combined French and Spanish fleet in the British Navy's finest hour, the Battle of Trafalgar, just within sight of Tangier. Nelson lost his life as a result of that battle but Moses Pariente did not lose his money. The British Admiralty honoured the I.O.U. and, being grateful, gave Pariente much of its local business therafter. It was the start of a great financial empire as Mr Pariente later used his good profits to open Tangier's first bank, the highly respected Moses Pariente which has now left Tangier but still operates from Geneva.

Nelson came out of it well also. When he died his body was secretly sent from Gibraltar to London in a large barrel full of brandy to stop him decomposing. The most macabre aspect of this, which rarely appears in history books, is that some of the ship's crew, unaware that Nelson's body was in the barrel, drilled a hole in it late one night and secretly siphoned out all the brandy which they drank. Perhaps this is how the phrase "getting dead drunk" originated ?

But Nelson's spirit would not have minded because massive Falklands type publicity about his victory made him the hero of the day back in the UK.

He was buried in St Paul's.

That incredibly high stone pillar was erected in Trafalgar Square with his statue proudly atop.

And, ever since, British historians and film makers have romantically cleansed his illicit affair with mistress (Lady) Hamilton by presenting it as "One of the world's greatest love stories".

Which just goes to show that with the media boys on your side, you can't go wrong.

As far as actual British presence in Tangier is concerned, that's about it. But for those who want to know more about the basic history of this city, it is probably the oldest continuously inhabited centre in Morocco. The known history goes back to before 1,000 B.C. when, along with two nearby sites, it was used as a trading post by the Phoenicians who came in peace and did little to disturb the Berber locals.

Then came the Carthaginian traders. After Carthage was destroyed by Rome in 146, the Romans swept through, followed in 429 by the Vandals and then the Turks. The Arabs came in 705 AD and 83 years later, Idris I, started the moves which eventually resulted in the Kingdom of Morocco.

The Portuguese captured Tangier in 1471, the English accepted it as that wedding dowry in 1661 and then withdrew, as previously stated, in 1684. In 1912 Morocco was made a French Protectorate with Spain governing smaller patches of the country such as Ceuta and Melilla.

In 1923 the Statute of Tangier formalised international control over the 140 square miles covering Tangier and its surroundings and the governing powers were Britain, France, Spain, Portugal, Holland, Sweden, Italy and Belgium. For the next 23 years Tangier was a boom city which became rich and world notorious as Sinville on Sea until Moroccan Independence in 1956 and then the big clean up started.

Colonial domination was slowly but surely wiped out and life undeniably improved for all Moroccans under the wise administration of His Majesty King Moulay Hassan II, who, since 1961, has carried on the work of his illustrious father, H.M. Mohammed V.

You Are In Good Company

There is some controversy as to whether SAINT FRANCIS OF ASSISI, one of childhood's favourite saints, came to Tangier or not. Some historians say he came here in 1216 but others deny it. Those who insist he did, claim that on leaving he described Tangier as "A city of madness and illusion". We leave it to you to judge whether he came or not.

ALEXANDRE DUMAS, the author of the Three Musketeers definitely came to Tangier in 1844 and a street was named after him. This might have been because while here he invented a tonic drink of Ambergris, chicken stock and sugar as a rejuvenator for tired, listless and lustless middle-aged husbands. If you want the recipe, Mabel, write to us at this adress : Iserra, Boite Postale 641, Tangier, and we will send it you free, with our condolences. Hurry, before it's too late.

HANS CHRISTIAN ANDERSEN, the Danish author, came to Tangier in 1863 and was fascinated by local fables and fairies, some of which he mentioned in his later stories. The fables, that is.

GASTON LEROUX, author of The Phantom of the Opera arrived in 1906 and was intrigued by Tangier's legendary ghost, Aisha Kandisha, though he did not manage to meet her.

The French composer SAINT SAENS lived in the Fuentes Hotel in the Petit Socco and NICOLAI RIMSKY-KORSAKOV was inspired to write his famous Sheherazade while sitting in the Place de la Kasbah next to the Old Sultan's Palace.

Many famous personalities have visited Tangier incognito for various reasons. One was MARK TWAIN, the American humourist who booked into a local hotel under his real name, Samuel Clemens, in 1867. After leaving he wrote that this city was "a foreign land if there ever was one".

DANIEL DEFOE, the author of Robinson Crusoe, came to Tangier searching for another Man Friday in 1715. He used the name Alexander Goldsmith and records in the British Museum disclose that under this and other names he received regular payments as a spy from British Secret Service Accounts during the previous year.

EUGENE DELACROIX, the French painter came here in 1832 and was so impressed by the unique effect of local light and colour that he expanded his technique and, according to experts, painted some of his best works in this city. His painting of a Tangier "Jewish Wedding" hangs in the Louvre.

HENRI MATISSE lived here for two years from 1911. Staying at the Villa de France Hotel he sat in Room 35 and painted his famous "View of Tangier Bay" which hangs in Grenoble Museum. Today, his admirers pay about £15 to stay overnight in that room.

JOHN LAVERY the noted Irish artist came to Tangier in 1893, built a studio on The Mountain and for 50 years painted there every winter. He achieved wide fame for his portraits of George Bernard Shaw, the ballerina Pavlova, the kidnapped Caid Maclean and WINSTON CHURCHILL.

Winston also painted here and in Marrakech. In 1958 Winnie stayed at the Rif Hotel which still has a generous letter of thanks from his wife, Clementine. Dated August 1958, she ended the letter by saying she thought Tangier was "a congenial and pleasant part of the world with a wonderful climate and full of local colour. I cannot imagine a more agreeable holiday resort". She and Winnie also stayed on the fabulous yacht owned by ARISTOTLE ONASSIS which anchored in the bay just opposite the Rif Hotel for more than a week.

Locals were amazed to discover that when Onassis pulled a pair of bull's horns mounted on the main deck, the dance floor slid away to reveal a heated swimming pool. The yacht also boasted a miniature submarine, two speed boats and a large landing craft. No wonder Onassis landed Jackie.

Many famous writers have visited Tangier. Among them were ALAN SILLITOE, IAN FLEMING, GORE VIDAL, BEVERLEY NICHOLS, TRUMAN CAPOTE, GERTRUDE STEIN, EVELYN WAUGH, CHRISTOPHER ISHERWOOD and EMLYN WILLIAMS. Another writer named Williams was Tennessee who conceived his "Camino Real" from the hustle and bustle of the Grand Socco. He also scribbled notes for his "Cat On A Hot Tin Roof" while sunbathing on the patio of the seafront Sun Beach. Bar. At one stage, TENNESSEE WILLIAMS occupied an apartment in the old Rue Pizarro where he wrote "Suddenly Last Summer".

That same apartment was later used by another WILLIAMS named KENNETH, famous for his "Carry On" comedy roles. Camp Kenneth stayed there as the guest of JOE ORTON, the brilliant British playright who made his name with "Loot" and "Entertaining Mr Sloane". Joe first visited Tangier in 1965 with his long-time lover and co-writer, KENNETH HALLIWELL.

They returned to this city for a lengthy stay in 1967 during which they made several good friends. Sadly, just 39 days after their return to London, Kenneth Halliwell beat Joe Orton to death with a hammer in their Islington flat and then swallowed 23 Nembutal tablets which killed him.

Another writer, who is also a famous film maker, came to Tangier on his famous research ship Calypso. In 1943 he was the co-inventor of the Aqua Lung, the underwater breathing apparatus which totally revolutionized exploration of the deep. Yes, none other than JACQUES COUSTEAU.

How many people remember MARGARET LANE ? She's the lady who wrote the superb life story of Edgar Wallace after being his private secretary. Maggie came to Tangier with her titled hubby, Huntingdon, and settled in a pretty Kasbah house where she wrote three novels based on this city. The great EDGAR WALLACE also visited Tangier. This was in 1907 when he was a reporter working on the British Daily Mail and he was sent over to write a news story about Raisuli's sensational kidnapping of Britisher Harry Caid Maclean.

Another good writer who came to Tangier is NOEL MOSTERT, the former shipping correspondent for the liberal Cape Times in South Africa. In 1947 he went to Canada and became Parliamentary Correspondent for United Press in Ottowa. Now a Canadian citizen, he wrote the famous Penguin book 'Supership' which is a brilliantly documented and frightening exposé of the pollution of the seas by massive oil tankers.
At the moment, Mr Mostert is compiling another book in his home on the Mountain which overlooks the sea he clearly loves.

As we have already seen, several famous American authors have visited Tangier. In fact, it was an American who wrote the first guide book to Morocco. Her name was EDITH WHARTON. Born in New York in 1862, she started writing at the age of 35 and churned out some 40 novels and travel books. At the time of her death in 1937, she was regarded as a leading figure in modern American literature.

Canny Edith came to Morocco in 1917 and, discovering there was no guide book to the country, banged one out entitled "In Morocco". A rather quaint title when you know that the lady spent only 30 days in Morocco. The truth is that her book was simply a daily diary of her impressions. Heady stuff mostly about colourful flowers, golden sand, leafy palms, the smell of camels, spices, herbs and people and how many "Natives, blacks, negroes, brown babies and white people" she saw.

What few facts there are in the book she admits drawing heavily from 23 books about Morocco written by Frenchmen who lived and worked here.

And intriguingly the French, whom she adored and always praised to the heavens, awarded her the Legion of Honour for her "relief work" during the First World War.

Well-connected Edith travelled round Morocco in a car driven by a hand-picked French military chauffeur and a French Army Captain bodyguard. Neither spoke one word of Arabic. Edith spent less than 24 hours in Tangier but, during that time, decided it was "Cuckoo-like, cosmopolitan, frowsy and familiar". She clearly didn't have the time to get very familiar with this city so we must presume it was the locals she found just a little too...

Another American who came to Tangier was the famous author ROBERT RUARK. He didn't fancy the city much either because he returned home to write that Tangier contained more "Spies, thieves, black marketeers, thugs, phonies, bums, beachcombers, degenerates, tramps and charlatans than any other place I have visited". It should be remembered that when Ruark wrote this, Tangier was under French rule. He was spot on about the spies though. During World War Two, this city was a neutral zone and it had plenty of them and they kept coming and going for years after the war.

NOEL COWARD, that droll, po-faced showbiz genius loved the unusually gay entertainment that tantalising Tangier provided and he worked not only for French Intelligence but also British Security as a top society gossip gatherer and rumour-spreading disinformation operative, though he modestly admitted later : "There's nothing much more to be said about that".

Another British spy was GUY BURGESS who, of course, turned out to be a KGB double agent. He came to Tangier in the Forties and got into trouble with the fourteens but, as that other top British spy and KGB double, Kim Philby indicates in his book "My Silent War", a bit of high level diplomacy was mounted by Whitehall and Burgess got away Scott free as JEREMY THORPE would have said. Jeremy came here in the Sixties but didn't bring Norman with him.

One of the best loved British agents was MARGARET ISOBEL "TEDDY" DUNLOP, who was the Vice Consul at the British Legation in Tangier. She also happened to be a highly efficient senior member of Britain's Secret Intelligence Service (SIS) and her husband, Doctor Harry Dunlop, a delightful Scot, is still fondly remembered in this city where he cured many poor Moroceans often without charge. Harry was also a British agent.

The most controversial British agent was Colonel WILLIAM "TOBY" ELLIS, a British Army doctor who had worked in South Africa and settled in Tangier in the Thirties where he became a successful whisky importer and later, a local correspondent for the British "Times". Ellis was so strict that he lost Randolph Gusus, his best Moroccan agent, to the Americans. Why ? Because Randolph made spelling mistakes when typing out his secret reports in English. After the war the Americans awarded Randolph the coveted American Medal of Freedom with Palm and publicly described him as "a priceless agent".

The most dangerous agent in wartime Tangier, from the Allied point of view, was KURT REITH, the local German Minister and Gestapo link man who had earlier arranged the shock assassination of Austrian Chancellor Engelbert Dollfus, for the Nazis. Reith's favourite drinking place was the bar at the Rif Hotel.

Perhaps the bravest British agent Tangier has known was A.W. "XAN" FIELDING, a travel writer who, for three years carried out courageous work organising the underground resistance in enemy-occupied Crete during WW2. He also operated underground in German-occupied France in 1944 and was arrested by the Gestapo. He managed to escape three hours before he was due to be shot and in spite of this scary experience, carried on with his underground activities for which he was awarded the D.S.O.

In 1956 Xan Fielding settled in Tangier and lived in the lovely house next to the main gate entrance to the Kasbah later bought by MARK GILBEY of the Gilbey's Gin family.

Xan was a very popular figure in this city and so was his wife, Daphne, the former Lady Weymouth who wrote a boring and title-littered autobiography entitled "Mercury Presides". She made up for it ten years later though when, in 1964, she wrote the "Duchess of Jermyn Street", an interesting, yet ladylike expose of Rosa Lewis who was London's most famous high society brothel keeper. Rosa, at the age of 16 was a kitchen scrubber who became the mistress of His Majesty King Edward VII. With the King's money and patronage she went on to open London's famous Cavendish Hotel in Jermyn Street opposite the back door of Fortnum and Mason.

Here, from 1902 to 1952, she provided classy harlots and nymphs for Members of Parliament, Cabinet Ministers, high-ranking military officers and members of the aristocracy. Not surprisingly, Rosa's brothel managed to escape the attention of Scotland Yard during all those 50 years. That's something for Christine Keeler to mull over.

As we gave already seen from the impressive adventures of the "mule turd" landmine pioneer GORDON BROWNE, the American Intelligence chaps did sterling work in Morocco during World War Two.

Another American agent worth extra mention is CARLETON COON, the anthropologist who found those famous bones at Tangier's Caves of Hercules. A former Harvard professor, Coon operated in Tangier and various other parts of Morocco, often in partnership with Gordon Browne.

In his autobiography, Coon tells the remarkable story of a local fisherman who worked as an information gatherer for the Americans and was codenamed Neanderthal. This man lived near the Caves of Hercules and possessed a permit from the Spanish which allowed him to fish along the coast.

But while fishing he kept his eyes open for anything that moved along the coastal road. He spied on all Spanish troop movements and quickly pinpointed a battery of anti aircraft guns when they were secretly hidden in the Phoenician remains just past the Caves of Hercules. Looking for the reason, this illiterate fisherman finally chanced upon the biggest "fish" of his career. The one that did not get away.

Although the Spaniards were allegedly neutral, their guns were used to protect a German submarine lurking in safety under the nearby cliffs. The sub regularly dashed from its hiding place and attacked Allied shipping passing through the Straits of Gibraltar. On receiving this valuable information from agent Neanderthal, the Americans transmitted it to British Intelligence in Gibraltar and the German sub was put out of action by a British fighter bomber after being lured out into the Straits by a false message. Local American agents recommended that agent Neanderthal should be rewarded by the British with a gift of 12 cows after the war but Whitehall refused. It's too late to give Neanderthal his cows now. He died at his home near the Caves of Hercules in 1984.

Enough of spies. Hundreds of famous film stars have enjoyed Tangier, the notables being Douglas Fairbanks, Victor Mature, Stanley Baker, Marlene Dietrich, (who came to make the film "Morocco"), Gary Cooper, who made "Beau Geste" and Humphrey Bogart who, of course made the film "Casablanca" in 1942 with Ingrid Bergman. Few people know that this film was actually filmed right here in Tangier's Kasbah, not Casablanca. The latest action film to be made in this city was the spy thriller "Tangier" in 1981. Ronald Fraser became a frequent visitor here after making that film. If you want to see it, go to the Rif Hotel where they have it on video.

That ancient Hollywood Tarzan Johnny Weissmuller suffered a nervous breakdown after visiting Tangier in 1958 and when staying at the El Minzah, John Gielgud did not feel good. But Joan Collins, Hattie Jacques, Alec Guinness, Anna Neagle and Harry Seacombe liked the city. So did Margaret Leighton and Lawrence Harvey who were married on a ferry in the Gibraltar Bay before steaming over here. Others who liked Tangier were Lord Montagu of vintage car and other fame, socialite photographer Cecil Beaton, T.S. Eliot the poet ; Francis Bacon the painter and Sidney Poitier, the Man Who Came For (More Than One) Dinner.

Mick Jagger of the Rolling Stones rolled into Tangier to get stoned in 1966 and had trouble with drugs, alleged possession of. Charles Aznavour sang for his supper at the now defunct Casino but Charles Blondin, the daring Frenchman who walked across Niagara Falls on a tightrope, stopping halfway to cook and eat an omelette, believe it or not, didn't fancy walking in our Kasbah.

The Richardsons came to Tangier and so did the two Kray brothers before being jailed in Britain for a gangland killing. Another Briton who dealt in death was Bill Moore who came here from Liverpool in 1959 when he was aged 26. Those of us who met him at the Cafe de Paris thought he was a quiet and rather shy individual. How wrong we were. Within a matter of weeks he met Barbara Muller, an attractive American girl aged 19 and murdered her after a chat on the Tangier beach. In August 1981, Moore was returned to Britain after serving 21 years in the Tangier Jail.

Rather different was Billy Hill, King of the London underworld in the Forties and Fifties. He set up a flat here and had no problems because he always behaved like a British gentleman though some local Brits snootily ignored him, saying he wasn't.

The German Kaiser was given a great procession through the Medina in March 1905 but left quickly as he feared being shot by a French hit squad in a plot which was never proven.

Another Royal of German background who came to Morocco was that debonair Greek-born Prince, Philip of Edinburgh. With him was his hard-working wife Elizabeth, who took photos of local scenes with her gold-plated Japanese Leica and then declined to eat the lovely local lobsters saying : "I never eat the awful looking things". Mind you, she's been ultra cautious since that famous visit to the South Pacific where she ate an unusually tasty dish only to be told afterwards that it was roast bat. Royal watchers might be interested to know that while in Morocco, the Prince and Queen disclosed that they never ate oysters. Maybe because they don't like to see them cringing away from the vinegar ?

The Queen drank gin and tonic at night and Prince Philip downed lager with scotch as a chaser. Before leaving, Queen Elizabeth gave the Moroccan people a really thoughtful and practical present. Ten British ambulances which, for some unknown reason, were modified by a firm on the Continent. One of these was allocated to the city of Tangier and it still speeds round town on missions of mercy just about every day.

Few people have heard of a rather different English lady who left her mark here. This was Mrs Maria Dickin, who founded the People's Dispensary for Sick Animals (P.D.S.A.) in London in 1917. In the Twenties she gave Morocco the very first overseas PDSA branch. Right here in Tangier.

Another English lady deserving mention is PAT PRIOR, born in Richmond, Surrey, who settled in Morocco in 1956. A midwife, she has delivered more than 1,800 Moroccan babies, often without charge when the family was poor. Pat now lives in Tangier where she works tirelessly for both church and charity.

Would You Settle Here?

This chapter is for Westerners who might consider living in Tangier permanently. The thought occurs to many because the city offers a much higher standard of living and, of course, we have those 350 days of sunshine every year almost without fail. January and February are usually the colder months but the sun shines through the clouds even when it rains and the temperature rarely falls below 12 degrees.

One unusual aspect of Tangier's weather is the wind that blows now and again. Westerners tend to refer to it as the Levanter but Moroccans call it the Sharqi, which is the correct pronunciation for the Arabic word Sharq, meaning the East.

In fact, Tangier has four winds and the dry, warm one creates some very strange electro-magnetic vibrations and tends to make some people nervous or bad tempered. On the other hand, it's not as bad as the Foehn wind in Switzerland which scientists have named the Wind of

Evil because it causes a dramatic increase in violent, even senseless, crimes just as the dry Sirocco wind that blows from the Libyan desert causes extremely unpleasant changes in human behaviour and judges in that part of the Mediterranean are often enlightened enough to impose very lenient sentences on normally well-behaved people who commit uncharacteristic crimes when that patience cracking wind blows.

Perhaps one day, a serious scientific study will be made of Tangier's winds and also of the folklore and herbal medicine men in this city who can recognise and cure certain nervous conditions by their amazing knowledge of our strange winds and their effect on different people.

If that does not put the wind up you and you are a businessman wishing to set up a factory in Tangier, make note of the fact that the Moroccan Government will give you free land on which to build it. But private individuals thinking of settling here should think carefully because Tangier really is a different world and it takes a very special breed of person to cope with the difference.

Do intensive research before selling up everything back home and making your move. Perhaps the wisest course is to come and live here in a rented apartment for three to six months. Only then will you really discover whether you can cope. If you like the city, a residence permit is not hard to obtain if you are of good character and can show you are financially sound.

Talking about money, perhaps the easiest way to import sizeable amounts is to open an account at the B.M.C.E. bank in the Free Zone area of Tangier's Port. The bank will advise you how to have your money telexed through and we suggest you open a Deposit Account for the bulk of your money which, in the Free Zone bank, can be kept in Dollars or Sterling. The bank pays a very good interest rate and this interest is automatically paid monthly into a small current account which the bank will also gladly open for you.

A good tip. Do not change your money on the Black Market. You might get a few Dirham more but it really is not worth it. Banks, hotels and approved cambios must, by law, give an exchange slip as a receipt bearing your name and passport number. These slips are vitally important when you apply for residence as they prove you are a responsible person.

Surprisingly, 306,000 British pensioners live overseas in the sun because their Old Age Pensions stretch much further, particularly in

Greece, Italy, Spain and Morocco. One pensioner who lives in Tangier is JOHN EDWARDS who is known to everyone as 'Gibraltar John' because he ran a small bar in Gib during the late Seventies. Reputed to be the smallest bar in the world, it held only 12 people. All standing. John made headlines when he was 13 and pinched the British Prime Minister's top hat. Pinched being rather a strong word as he was delivering newspapers and noticed the hat on a window ledge above the dustbins. The Premier's maid had put it out to air after wet brushing it but John presumed it had been thrown out so he plonked it on his head and wore it for the rest of the day until the Special Branch Odd Lot sussed him out and sent uniformed police to grab it back. The following Sunday, the News of the World ran a funny story about the young titfer snatcher who had decided that to get ahead he needed a hat.

As a Sergeant in the Royal Armoured Corps, John was blown up by a landmine during the liberation of Belgium. The blast broke both his legs, both arms, fractured his jaw and blew off one of his fingers. After running his bar in Gib, John retired to Tangier in 1980 because, as he rightly says, where else could a man live comfortably, as well as smoke and drink, on an Old Age Pension and Disability Pension of just 55 quid weekly after tax ?

Tangier has about 100 American residents and just over 200 full time British residents, plus about 60 British floaters who stay on and off. Most of them are older or retired as this city is not really a place for the young because finding work is not easy unless you have two or three languages and, in any case, a work permit is necessary.

Yet if you settle here with young children, have no fear about their education. They can attend the American School of Tangier (A.S.T.) which was founded in 1950. This private school is open to boys and girls of all religious and racial backgrounds and is situated on 16 prime acres in a quiet part of town though only a 10 minute walk from central Tangier.

The AST holds several well-attended functions every year, some of which are organised by its enthusiastic Parents' Committee. The school takes boarders and there's no finer place for English-speaking youngsters to learn languages. As far as High School students are concerned, the AST has an outstanding record of university placement in America. Recent graduates, many with full scholarships, have been awarded admission to Harvard, Yale, Penn, Bryn Mawr, Kenyon and the University of California at Berkeley.

The Headmaster of the AST is JOSEPH 'JOE' MCPHILLIPS III, a Princeton graduate who first started teaching at the AST in 1962 and was appointed Head in 1973. He is very popular with his students who like his casual, friendly manner and, with the help of his private secretary and an excellent team of teachers, runs a good and disciplined ship on the sometimes difficult to navigate sea of education.

Britishers who settle here can keep up to date with The Archers by tuning into Gibraltar Radio which might make them feel even more at home because it broadcasts regular daily record requests from The Falklands as well as many BBC link programmes. Gib TV can be picked up clearly in Tangier and runs popular soap operas such as Dallas and The Sullivans as well as Saturday night British movie specials.

You can enjoy excellent sports and cultural programmes on both Spanish and Moroccan TV which, refreshingly, do not feature so much porn, violence, bare boobs and capped teeth.

If you bring a car to Tangier it can only stay for six months in any year but you can apply for Moroccan registration if you pay tax on the vehicle. Westerners should be alert when driving here because Tangier has a unique breed of jay walkers who seem to love giving drivers apoplexy. On the other hand, Moroccan drivers are good and statistics show that Morocco, on vehicle ratio and population comparison, has one of the lowest road death tolls in the world. The fact that Moroccans do not drink liquor also helps.

This does not mean you should relax your vigilance when walking round Tangier. Westerners really should learn to look both ways before crossing streets. Even one-way ones. On another humourous note, should you buy a car in Tangier, make sure it is not a small green one or you will find yourself being flagged down all the time by people who think you are a Petit Taxi.

As far as Tangier's future is concerned, local businessmen are extremely optimistic. They firmly believe that in the very near future it will once again become a boom city. Several snippets of information appear to support this.

All over town you will notice new houses and modern apartment blocks being constructed. This is in spite of the fact that there is no shortage of quality housing.

142

Tangier's Voice of America radio relay station is being expanded at a cost of about 200 million dollars and on completion will be one of the most powerful in the world with ten transmitters each having an output power of 500 kilowatts. Situated at Briech, 10 km from Asilah on the Tangier to Rabat road, the station will cover 450 hectares and will be broadcasting in 25 languages.

A modern marina costing over seven million dollars-is underway on the Malabata side of Tangier Bay and it is hoped this will lure the many private yachts and sailing craft owned by the rich Mediterranean Set which has long wanted to use Tangier as a cheaper home base.

In February 1985 it was disclosed that a 100 million dollar company was being formed to set up a giant fishing and refrigeration business in Tangier's Zone Franche. That's the Free Zone area in the port. Further confidence in Tangier's future is proved by the fact that many oil-rich billionaires in Kuwait and Saudi Arabia have bought and are still buying beautiful properties in and around this city.

His Majesty King Fahd of Saudi Arabia probably started this trend when he built a picturesque palace in the Mountain section of this city. And another rich man from the Middle East is reported to have bought the old white walled prison on the Malabata side of the bay, just past the Tariq Hotel, with the intention of building a holiday home there.

It is no secret that several oil rich countries in the Middle East would like to bank their billions here. Sticking money in Threadneedle Street vaults and buying prime properties such as London's Dorchester Hotel may still continue but Tangier seems the obvious answer to those Middle East billionaires who do not wish to have their money in a Western country where political or economic sanctions could possibly be imposed and where they know that their accounts are open to scrutiny from prying eyes which secretly have access to the London-based computors used by Britain's Big Five banks.

All that Middle East gold will almost certainly come to Tangier if this city becomes an International Free Port again. And that is the biggest talking point in Tangier at the moment. The highly respected JOURNAL DE TANGER started the ball rolling by pointing out that Tangier has the know how and the perfect geographical position. If there's one thing this city knows, it's how to handle money. In the old days when Tangier was a Free Port it boasted no less than 84 banks. And that was when the city was only half the size it is today.

143

Four million people cross the Straits of Gibraltar every year, mainly landing at Tangier or Ceuta and to cater for this vast traffic, a gigantic 3,000 million dollar project is underway to dig a 30 km long undersea tunnel from the Eastern Malabata side of Tangier to near Algeciras in Spain. This might take ten years to complete but when it is, the driving time from Spain to Tangier will be about 25 minutes.

The least known but most thought provoking titbit is that the United Nations has long considered leaving America and bringing itself lock, stock and barrel to Tangier. This makes sense as the UN would thus be more accessible to the great majority of its delegates, particularly the European, Arab and African ones. Some say the possibility of the UN coming here is rather wishful thinking, but Tangier businessmen are keeping their fingers crossed as they know it would result in this city becoming a fantastic boom area where property values would rocket overnight.

More Information Sources

If your appetite has been whetted and you would like to read more about Tangier, here is a list of books consulted by The Rogue's Guide but which you can consider according to taste.

SECOND SON, published by Peter Owen 1972, is an autobiography by David Herbert who is known as a social lion in Tangier. He can be seen every Sunday at the English Church where he acts as Consular Warden, showing local Consuls and others to their seats. An Old Etonian, ex-film actor, one-time night club singer and the second son of the Earl of Pembroke, the Hon David Herbert has lived in Tangier since 1950 and has acted as host to an avalanche of titled or rich personalities. He names most of them in this gentle, often amusing book, which is a must for all socialites, but not Socialists.

THE WRONG PEOPLE by Robin Maugham. Heinemann 1970. A brilliant novel set in Tangier and which really brings the city to life. It is said to be based on a real life case in which a young boy was semi-kidnapped from a British approved school. A must for anyone wishing to understand male homosexuals and their unique problems in life and love. Somerset Maugham advised his nephew Robin not to write this book under his real name "or they will murder you", so.he published it under the pen name of David Griffin when it first surfaced via Paperback Library in 1967.

REBELS IN THE RIF by David Woolman 1969. A good historical breakdown containing a condensed history of Morocco. It met with criticism from some people who claimed Woolman's pen was too bitter.

TANGIER, A DIFFERENT WAY also by David Woolman but written under the anagram pen name of Lawdom Vaidon and published by Scarecrow Press USA 1978. A more thorough history of Tangier which, half way through, contains spicy gossip picked up by Woolman when he worked here as a journalist. This book was attacked by some British and American residents who were mentioned by name and you will not find a copy of it on sale in Morocco.

TANGIER, A WRITER'S NOTEBOOK by Angus Stewart, Hutchinson 1977. An unusual autobiography partly based on the author's homosexuality. Candid, perceptive and often brilliant.

THE KHALIFATE OF THE WEST by Donald McKenzie 1911, tells of the author's 25 years in Morocco. This handsome Scot first came to Tangier in 1875. Later he set up a trading post at Cape Juby where some romantics claim he created Morocco's famous Blue People by selling to the desert nomads a cotton cloth dyed blue with a cheaper type of indigo which rubbed off on to their skins and stayed there.

ADVENTURES AND DISCOVERIES is the egobiography of the famous American anthropologist Carleton Coon published by Prentice Hall in 1981. It's a great pity that this famous man overstates his successes and knocks down those of his close associates because, as a big actor on the stage of life, he hated being upstaged. If you believe Coon, he was the best American secret agent in Morocco and the first to walk across the Straits of Gibraltar.

TANGIER. UN SIECLE D'HISTOIRE. A factual paperback in French about the last 100 years in Tangier's history with 120 old photographs. Written by local real estate agent Isaac Assayag and on sale at Sapit, the efficient stationery shop in the arcade next to Le Claridge at 54 Bvd Pasteur.

WIT AND WISDOM IN MOROCCO by Edward Westermarck 1931. This book is a must for collectors. It is a really superb 448-pager full of delightful and thought provoking Moroccan proverbs. The best book ever written in Morocco and the perfect present for that millionaire who claims he has everything. If you find a copy in a junk shop, grab it.

COUS COUS AND OTHER FOODS FROM MOROCCO by Paula Wolfert, Harper and Row 1973. Paula is a tall, intense brunette from New York who spent several years in Morocco. Her book is splendid.

MOROCCAN COOKING, THE BEST RECIPES by Fettouma Benkirane is said to be the best paperback cook book for tourists. Obtainable from Colonnes Bookshop, 54 Bvd Pasteur.

71 DAYS CAMPING IN MOROCCO by Lady Agnes Grove, London 1902. A bit old fashioned but the hilarious title has made it a collector's item in some camps.

PEPSIANA by H.B. Wheatley 1899, exposes Samuel Pepys by publishing those bits of his famous diaries that other editors left out.

THE ROUGH GUIDE TO MOROCCO edited by Mark Ellingham, Routledge and Kegan Paul 1985. Costs about 80 Dirham. Rather weak on Tangier but strong on Moroccan history and culture.

THE KORAN. English edition, Penguin Books 1956, is the book we recommend for readers seeking religious information. The Koran is the earliest and by far the finest work of Classical Arabic prose. For Muslims it is the infallible word of Allah, a transcript of a tablet preserved in Heaven, revealed to the PROPHET MOHAMMED by the Angel Gabriel.

Dr Raschad Khalima, the Imam at the Islamic Mosque in Tucson, Arizona, believes that The Koran holds the key to the secret of the universe. He has fed The Koran into a computor and what came out was a mysterious, complex and regular repetition of the figure 19. The first verse of the first sura has 19 letters. Each single word in this first line reappears in The Koran a number of times which is divisible by 19. The computor gave hundreds of such strange coincidences and the odds against this, says Dr Khalima, is thousands of billions to one.

THE ETERNAL MESSAGE OF MOHAMED, obtainable at Colonnes Bookshop, is excellent for those needing full background information on Mohammed the Prophet who died in June 632,

The Founder of Islam, Mohammed was chosen by Allah in 610 as a messenger of the new word and as a Prophet. The simple appeal of Mohammed's message, embodied in the Koran, won acceptance and welded the tribes of Arabia into unity but wisely left the conquered people to manage their own affairs.

In Islam there is no intermediary between man and God in the form of an institutionalised priesthood or complicated liturgy. And worship, in the form of prayer, is a personal and direct communication with God. Believers face five essential requirements which are known as the Pillars of Islam or the Pillars of Faith. They are :

Prayer five times daily.

The pilgrimage to Mecca.

The Giving of Alms.

The acceptance that there is no God but God and Mohammed is his Prophet.

The Ramadan fast.

RAMADAN is the very special Holy Month during which Allah revealed The Koran to Mohammed. During this 30 day period, Muslims allow no food or drink to pass their lips from dawn to dusk. The aged, the young, the ill, travellers and the pregnant are excused. Tourists who eat, drink and smoke at cafes in town during the daylight hours of Ramadan are advised to do so as unobstrusively as possible and Moroccans really appreciate this. In any case it's a matter of simple politeness as a guest in a host country.

THE LAST WORD

Well, that's about it. We hope you have enjoyed the Rogue's Guide and we also hope the A to Z Need to Know List and the Index at the end prove useful. We have tried to include everything which could be of general interest to tourists visiting Tangier but, as every writer knows full well, you can't please everyone. Whatever you write, someone always complains or jumps out of a cave grunting contradictions.

Take Tangier's ancient history for instance. The truth is that hardly anything is known about it, though many books have tried to cover the subject. Proof of this is that some historians claim that the lost continent of Atlantis is located where the Atlantic meets the Med. Others deny it.

Some historians say the Gardens of The Hesperides rested on the Atlantic shore near Larache, but this has also been denied.

Legend tells us that the Phoenician word for swamp was Ting and, as the shores all round this area were mostly swampland when they arrived, they named it Tingi which later became Tingis, then Tangier.

Yet this is contradicted by historians who say Tingis was the name given by the Romans. Yet another legend has it that Noah gave Tangier its name after he sent a dove to find land. When it returned to the Ark it had mud on its beak. Noah is alleged to have shouted "The mud has arrived" which, in his tongue, was pronounced Tinjda and he came ashore to discover Tangier.

More romantic is the legend claiming that the Greek hero Hercules met a beautiful woman in this area, that her name was Tanja and he named Tangier after her. Scientists say that Africa and Europe were parted by an earthquake but legend claims that Hercules did it by tearing apart the peaks of Gibraltar and Morocco's twin mountain, Jebel Musa. These two peaks, known as the Pillars of Hercules, are definitely similar, as you will see if you take the coastal road to Ceuta. Did old Hercules tear them apart though ? If he did, he must have been at least 25,000 feet tall. Yet that does not fit the famous footprint of Hercules in the large boulder by the roadside near Cap Spartel on the Atlantic Coast. According to that alleged footprint, Hercules was only about 75 feet in height.

This all goes to show that you can't be sure about history or legends and makes you wonder whether those historians were potty old eccentrics or just made mistakes.

Ah, well, they say it's human to err. Nobody is perfect, as the nude actress said to the defrocked Bishop. And reaching perfection when you write a book about Tangier is not at all easy because this is a city where, if you ask one simple question, you can often get six different answers. Three of them being correct, depending on the thought processes of the people answering.

We have tried our best not to make serious errors in this book but, as a little teaser for the observant Westerners who live here, we have made one deliberate mistake

The Rogue's Guide makes no pretence of being a literary masterpiece, so the professional critics can put their magnifying glasses away. It was deliberately written in an amusing and matey style because we felt that an informative, simple to read, yet entertaining guide to this complex city was sorely needed. Especially by Westerners who have never visited an Arabic country before.

We have taken great care not to write anything unkind about any person living in Tangier and, in fact, every living person mentioned at length has confirmed all our comments, either in their own writings, or to us personally before publication.

In an attempt to avoid errors of judgment, we asked 16 people who are well informed about Tangier, or have specialist knowledge on certain aspects, to proof-read our manuscript. In alphabetical order they are :

Fraser Anderson and Pamela ; Linda Armstrong ; Robert Barnete ; Don Collins ; Barrie Crees ; Webb Ellis ; Ronnie Fraser ; Dorothy Leyburn ; Margaret Oddy ; Joan Pearson ; the two Robb brothers ; Isabel Serra ; Tony Stratton-Smith and Eric Walker.

We also submitted our first draft to Mr Abdellah Taheri of the OFFICIAL TOURIST OFFICE who sent a summary to Rabat. Clearly then, we have gone out of our way to be accurate and fair to all sides. We spell that out just in case someone jumps out of a cave and starts grunting contradictions or complaining that a comma is missing (blame that on the gremlins in the printing works, mate).

On a more serious note, the small items of medical information in this book were supplied by reputable doctors and chemists. But it is always wise for people in poor health, or those suffering allergies, to double check any problems, however minor, with a doctor. If, however, you decide to use the information yourself, then you are prescribing for yourself, which is your democratic right for which the authors and printers assume no responsibility. We mention this because in Spain last year a reputable British travel firm recommended an excellent tablet manufactured by a world famous company. One woman who took the tablet became ill because she was a one in a million exception who was allergic to something in the tablet. The travel firm was so concerned by this that it quickly issued instructions to all its staff that no medicine should be prescribed to anyone without the backing of a doctor.

In Chapter Three we promised to give the the rules of the game PARCHESI, which originated in China 1,000 years ago. The rules vary slightly from city to city but we give you those which make the game particularly exciting. The suggestion that Parchesi is too difficult for British brains is nonsense. Our nine-year-old picked them up quicker than we did.

First of all, when you throw the dice it must land on the glass. To start, you must throw a five. Let's presume you are Red. In that case you start on slot number five. That's the red slot between 4 and 6. You travel round the board until you reach slot number 67. Then you go home down the private red avenue where nobody else can travel. As you go round the board you can be knocked off and sent back to starting base. But you cannot be knocked off if you are sitting on a Safe House. These are the black coloured slots with a white circle.

You cannot be knocked off while sitting on your own coloured doorstep but you can knock off other people if they land on your doorstep and you throw a coming out five.

To make the game more fun, every player shouts the word "OUT" when you throw a five. If you have a man in your starting base you must bring a man out. You have no choice. Whenever you throw a six you move six spaces forward. But if you have all four of your men out you must move 12 spaces. You have no choice. If you cannot move 12 spaces forward you can move six but forfeit the free throw which you get every time you throw a six. If you throw six three times in a row, the last man you moved is sent back to starting base as a penalty. But if his last move caused him to land on a safe house then he does not have to go back to base.

You can keep two of your men on any slot if you wish and by doing so you create a barrier which nobody can pass. But if you have such a barrier and you throw a six, everyone shouts "Break Your Barrier" and you must do so by moving one of the men forward. If you knock someone off you are rewarded by being allowed to move any one of your men 20 slots forward. If there is a barrier in the way you cannot use the 20 free moves. And if you are less than 20 slots from home you cannot take the 20 free moves.

You can land on the doorstep of another players' starting base even if he has a man sitting there and by doing so you form a barrier which cannot be passed by anyone. But this is a barrier which must be broken if either of you throw a six.

If you have two barriers and you throw a six you can choose which barrier to break first. If two other men are sitting on your coloured starting slot and you throw a coming out five then both the other men are knocked off and you get a free 40 moves forward, as long as no barrier is in the way of your progress. Once you reach your private going home avenue you must throw the exact number required to get home. Whenever you get a man completely home you may move any one of your other men ten spaces forward as a premium.

Parchesi is a very sporting game and in Morocco the loser pays for tea or coffee. But if there is any argument during play and you have no supporting witness then you toss a coin to decide who is correct.

O.K., that's the end of the rules of Parchesi. But the book does not actually end here because, on the next page, there is a Need to Know List which contains many extra valuable snippets of information. After that comes the fingertip Index.

ENJOY YOUR HOLIDAY

Need to Know List

This Need to Know List contains valuable extra information, in alphabetical order. It is not the index. That comes at the end of the book.

BAIT for fishing. Street vendors sit at the bottom of those 43 stone steps just past the El Minzah Hotel.

BANKS. Open from about 8-30am to 11-30am and 2-30pm to 4-15pm or 4-30. They close Saturday and Sunday. Banks do not change Dirham back into Sterling or Dollars etc. This can only be done on your departure day at the port or airport and even then you need to show exchange slips proving that you changed money into Dirham during your holiday in Morocco.

BOOKS. Colonnes Bookshop at 54 Bvd Pasteur is famous. Many in English. Fixed price. For secondhand paperbacks in good condition for about 5 Dirham, visit Fatima who runs the pretty little boutique on the mezzanine floor of the El Minzah Hotel. For dusty hardbacks and paperbacks try the junk shop at 49 Rue Omar Ibn Alhass, the street opposite the Hotel Chellah's front door.

BULL RING. Opposite the Pasadena Hotel, but the ring is now closed.

BUSES. In this city most roads lead to the Grand Socco and so do the buses. If you are walking from a beachfront hotel, look for the blue and white bus stops bearing the numbers 5, 15 or 21 and the words "Place du 9 Avril" which is the official name for the Grand Socco. Buses are efficiently run and fares are very cheap.

CAMERA REPAIRS and reasonably priced film. Ask for Ramish, the owner of the Isardas shop at 30 Bvd Pasteur. For film developing try Studio Flash three doors down from the El Minzah or, if time is of the essence, Studio Samar in Bvd Pasteur, opposite Algemene Bank, because they process and print in 45 minutes.

CAMPING. Of the caravan type. Try the Miramonte motel and caravan park on the Marshan hillside near Merkalla Beach. German-trained staff. Sleeping baggers also catered for. Another caravan park is the Tingis on the Malabata side of town. If you want to camp in the country yet still have beaches nearby, try the site at Hercules Grottoes across the road from the Mirage Restaurant. For young campers and sleeping baggers who want way out disco on the beach until 4am, look under the entry YOUNG SET.

CAR HIRE. Avis and Hertz, but smaller and cheaper firms exist. Check the petrol. Refuse any dirty or damaged car. Take out extra insurance for a few Dirham as this buys psychological reassurance. Some firms accept a credit card instead of a cash deposit. You can arrange this with your travel rep more often than not.

CAR REPAIRS. We highly recommend British-trained Mohamed at the CHELBAT GARAGE at 28 Rue Hassan Dakhil, down the hill from the American School of Tangier. Phone English-speaking Mohamed at 439-17 and he will probably send a car to pick you up.

CONSULATES. The BRITISH are in the courtyard of Trafalgar House in Rue Amerique du Sud, opposite Dean's Bar down past the El Minzah Hotel. The AMERICANS are in Rue el Ouachaq ; GERMANS at 47 Ave Hassan II ; FRENCH opposite the Cafe de Paris ; SPANIARDS at Ave Sidi Bouabib ; ITALIANS at 35 Rue Ibn Al Farrat ; SWISS and DANES are above Rubis Grill, opposite Madame Porte ; PORTU-GUESE on the top floor of Coficom ;   SWEDES at 31 Ave Prince Heritier and the BELGIANS are at 124 Ave Sidi Mohammed Ben Abdellah.

DENTISTS. Mohamed Jrondi speaks English, is Paris-trained and has the latest modern equipment at 41 Bvd Pasteur opposite Le Claridge. If you prefer a dentist of the old school, English-speaking Mr J. de las Peñas is in Avenue Prince Heritier next door to the Cafe de France.

DOCTORS. Most package tour operators have their own doctor on call. Our doctor is Fraser Anderson, a delightful Scot who has practised here since 1934. Midday surgery. Phone 353-44. It costs extra if a doctor visits you at your hotel but who cares ? Your health insurance pays for everything. But don't forget to keep doctor's bill and receipts for medicines which you must submit to your travel company when you return home.

DRY CLEANING. Detroit Pressing run by jovial Sheriff Temsemani at 10 Rue el Jaraoui, just across the road from the Cafe de Paris. Efficient service. The price list is on the electricity fuse box on your left as you enter and gives no shocks. Another good cleaner is Paris Pressing next to the Hotel Ritz just behind Madame Porte's tea salon.

ELECTRICITY. The current can be 110 or 220. Some hotels have both in bedrooms and bathrooms so check before plugging in. Don't leave your hair dryer or electric razor plugged in when not in use as we have power surges in Tangier and these can cause damage.

EMERGENCY CHEMIST. Every pharmacy has a card in the window or on the door which tells you where to go when they are closed. A particularly good emergency chemist is at 22 Rue de Fez in the arcade opposite Cinema Paris.

EYE PROBLEMS. English-speaking Georges Hermitte at RAVAS-SARD, 84 Rue de la Liberté, just across from the Café de Paris, sells spectacles and sunglasses you can trust. Speedy repairs and free eyesight tests. But ask for Georges Hermitte.

FANTASIA. We love it. A totally different scene consisting of robed riders firing rifles followed by a four course dinner in large Arabian tents with live cabaret of snake charmers, belly dancers, fire eaters, a Fakir on a bed of nails and camel rides. It's at the efficiently run Ahlen Village holiday complex. Get your tickets from your travel rep and enjoy a free bus ride there and back.

GOLF. Royal Country Club, 4 km from the city centre. 18 holes from 7am to sundown. Clubs and caddies can be hired. A good tip. Book your taxi for the return trip and save time.

HAIRDRESSERS. Three to consider. SALON JEAN (pronounced John) is very swish and is on the first floor at 23 Moussa Ben Noussair, just behind Madame Porte's tea salon. Or the hair stylist at the SOLAZUR HOTEL who is popular with many package tourists. Or try the polite, English-speaking Spaniard named PEPE who has a great following at his salon next to the Hotel El Minzah.

HOTELS for overnight trippers. Try the MIRAMAR on the beachfront or the British-run EL MUNIRIA in Rue Magellan. Both cost about £5 a night. The HOTEL CONTINENTAL, overlooking the port is slightly less. For cheaper nights try one of the many Pensions in Rue Salah Eddine el Ayoubi, opposite the railway station, or in town and also the Grand Socco and Petit Socco.

LIBRARY. Many British and American residents are members of the TANGIER BOOK CLUB, but tourists can take out books if they pay a small one month membership and give a refundable deposit. It's housed in the OLD AMERICAN LEGATION in Rue Amerique. The white door bell is high up out of kid's reach. Ring twice between 9-30am and noon and friendly GRAEME STEEL answers but not Sunday or Monday.

LEGATION. Old American, as above, is the oldest property owned on foreign soil by the U.S. Dept of State. A must for all Americans. Dr Robert Smith Shea, or a member of his staff will gladly give you a free walkabout tour. Scots will appreciate the special room set aside for the display of etchings by Scots-born JAMES MCBEY who lived in Tangier for over 40 years. His charming widow Marguerite, herself a painter with talent, still lives in this city.

LITHAM. A modesty veil which some call a yashmak.

MASSAGE. At the Rif Hotel every day. Ladies who are shy can have a massage and sauna with their husbands or girl friends. Ditto shy men.

PATRON SAINT OF TANGIER is Mohammed Bou Arrakia who died in 1718.

PHOTOSTATS. Many shops make them but we like GRAFICAS NORTE, a good stationery shop opposite the Cinema Goya, behind Madame Porte. At this shop you can also get brown paper for parcels. Any size you like is cut out by a clever string guillotine.

POST OFFICE. In Bvd Mohammed Five. Register all parcels you send home. An assistant in the rear parcels section will wrap your parcels and help you get them through customs. Don't seal your registered letters until the post office clerk has checked the contents.

POPULATION. In line with the copulation explosion everywhere else in the world, Tangier has a regular population of over 400,000 compared to 166,000 in 1961. In the Summer, Tangier plays host to over one million. Morocco has a population of about 24 million living in an area of 171,953 square miles of which, 32 per cent is used for agriculture, the main products being Barley, Wheat, Citrus Fruits, Vegetables, Sugar Beet and Wool. Major products are Textiles, Fish, Chemicals and Leather. Major natural resources are Phosphates, Iron, Manganese, Lead and Fisheries. Major trading partners are France, West Germany and Italy. Major exports are Phosphates, Fruit, Vegetables, Canned Fish, Carpets and Leather.

RELIGION. The English Church of St Andrews is in Rue d'Angleterre, three minutes walk from the El Minzah Hotel. British residents turn up in force for the 11am Sunday Service. When the church is closed, the Moroccan caretaker, Mustapha Cherqui, will gladly get out his keys and give you a free walkabout tour during which he discreetly points out the collection box. Notice the Lord's Prayer carved in Arabic script from right to left round the pretty chancel arch. The American Church is at 34 Rue Hassan Ibn Ouezzane ; the Italian Church is in Rue Moulay Driss ; the Catholic Church is in Rue Washington and the Jewish Synagogue, Chaar Raphael, is at 27 Bvd Pasteur, next to the Official Tourist Office.

MOSQUES. Non-Moslems are not allowed inside. Do not take photographs through doors or windows or of worshippers entering. A Mosque is where thought flows and flowers. Keep off the grass.

RIDING. There is the elegant Equestria Club but for those who like to ride wearing blue jeans there is the Ahlen Village complex and the Arabian Sands Holiday Club.

SHOPPING. Shops are open from early morning to about 1pm. Then, after Siesta, from about 3pm to 8pm. Friday is the Moslem Sabbath and some close. Saturday is the Jewish Sabbath, few close. Most shops in town close on Sunday though many remain open in the Kasbah. Bacals, those little grocery stores, provide a seven day service selling basic essentials such as bread, cold drinks, groceries and cigarettes (if you smoke).

STATIONERY. Sapit, in the arcade next to the Colonnes Bookshop at 54 Bvd Pasteur. Sapit also sell useful gifts and leather items with a touch of class.

TELEPHONE. Package tourists should experience no difficulties because hotel switchboard operators dial all calls for them. Campers and back packers can use the telephone in any bacal if they wish to make local calls (dial 10 or 12 to get an operator but few speak English). Campers who wish to make overseas calls will find it far more convenient to use the special phone boxes in the post office which are fully automatic and supervised by multi-lingual operators who not only have all dialling codes at their fingertips but also give official receipts for all cash payments.

TELEPHONE BOOK. When searching for a Westerner listed in the Tangier directory you might just find him, or her, listed under his (or her) first name. But then again you might not. Some of our friends who have been long dead are still listed. We are alive and well but our phone is not listed. You will get no heavy breathing calls here but you will often get the "Hello" caller. If you answer the phone with a hello, he will say hello back. Say hello again and so will he. Our record is 23 maddening hello's -- but, of course, it's our fault. The number of the local psychiatric hospital, by the way, is 388-07.

TELEVISION and Radio repairs. ELECTRONIC RADIO at 14 Rue Emsallah where the owner, Abslam Barmaki, knows his onions because he worked for R.C.A. for over 20 years. Another good firm is the ELECTRONIC CENTRE at 9 Rue Ibn Rochd, the small street opposite the Rembrandt Hotel. If you are watching Gibraltar TV and the sound goes, don't kick the set, the Gib TV commentator will eventually wake up and re-adjust the off-sync cassette after blandly lying his head off by telling you it was due to "a technical problem with the transmitter". Have you noticed that it's always a problem (ours not theirs) and never a FAULT ?

TIPPING is a way of life here but only if you get good service. 20 to 40 Centimes for a cafe waiter, depending on his speed and attentiveness. Tip a taxi well if he switched on his meter, a bootblack if he pleased you and a tip up front on your first day gets extra special service from hotel waiters in the dining room and also the chambermaids. A shrewd tip, that.

TOYS. Try TANGIER SPORTS opposite the El Minzah Hotel where they also sell the latest designed crutches - which is surprising because, import duty considered, the price of toys here is hardly crippling. For old fashioned and unusual toys try the fascinating BAZAR FRANCO-INGLES in the cul de sac at 32 Rue de la Liberté, run by Moses Lasry.

WATCH REPAIRS. Depending on the value of your watch, try the high class MADRID-PARIS clock shop in Ave Prince Héritier opposite the Mauritania Cinema or the clever young chap named Mohamed who sits at a soap box table between the freelance plumbers and the lottery ticket office in the Grand Socco.

YACHT CLUB. (On the beach). Not open to the public but tourists can arrange a special short membership during the Summer season. Ring the bell and have a look round first.

YACHT CLUB in the Port area. Membership only.

YOUNG SET. Camp Africa at Asilah, 45 km from Tangier, is popular with youngsters up to 30. Run by Scots-born Hamish Donaldson it is a fun place which offers cycles and surfboards for hire, horse riding, beach games, sensibly priced drinks and a video bar on the beach. Sleeping baggers pay about £1 nightly for a thatched roof hut. Phone Asilah (091) 7137.

Quick answers to most other questions can be found by using the fingertip INDEX which starts on the next page.

Index

Thanks to You All

For the title of this book we are indebted to David Joroff, alias Rogov, of Brooklyn, U.S.A. Other help came from Driss Ghazi, a gentleman journalist on the Journal de Tanger and our valued friend Mehdi 'Michael' Ben Moussa.

For educating us about the KORAN and MOHAMMED THE PROPHET we gratefully thank Abdelghani Alem, Mohamed Lechehab of the Dutch Bank and Brahim Cherkaoui of Etei-Nord.

For putting us on the right wavelength when we first arrived in Tangier, many thanks go to Hamed Amghar, the international radio ham (call sign C.N.2. A.H.) and his wife, Marlene.

Other Tangier specialists who gave valuable advice were :

Simon Cohen, the manager of the Rif Hotel (sorry I was so unmanageable, Simon) ; Martin Soames ; Tony Grimsdale ; Nigel Logan ; Jon King ; Brian Bird ; Trevor Palmer ; Ron Stewart ; Rosemary 'Romy' Connors ; Pamela and Alfons Runde ; Jelloul 'Mark' el Goumri ; Mohamed Chakkour Laroussi ; Katherine Soudi ; Jamayel ; Blanca ; Audrey ; Dilys ;Miguel ; Danny ; Cheekie ; Fouad and Abdellatif Ouarzazi, the whizz kid printer who compu-printed this book and rapped our knuckles gently when we missed errors in the galley proofs.

Last but not least, a million thanks to all those streetsmarts who often made us smart but never smarter.

ENDSIT

Imprimé sur les presses
ETEI-NORD
Zone Industrielle - Route de Tétouan
B.P. 101 - Tanger - (Maroc)
Décembre 1985

Photo-composition and printing by ETEI-NORD
Zone Industrial - Road to Tetouan - Tangier - (Morocco)